Now What?

Dr. Lonnie Johnson, Jr.

GAZELLE
PRESS

Faith Came—Now What?
by Dr. Lonnie J. Johnson, Jr.
Copyright ©2004 Dr. Lonnie J. Johnson Jr.

ISBN 1-58169-169-6
For Worldwide Distribution
Printed in the U.S.A.

FAITH CAME

Introduction

There is no other word in the Bible that is subject to more misunderstandings, deformities, and questionable definitions than the word "faith." It is one of those terms which need healing before they can be used for the healing of men. To illustrate, let me use a story credited to the *Christian Herald*.

Seeing and Believing

Two children were playing on a hillside, when they noticed the hour was nearing sunset, and one said wonderingly "See how far the sun has gone! A little while ago it was right over that tree, and now it is low down in the sky.

"Only it isn't the sun that moves; it's the earth. You know, Father told us," answered the other.

The first one shook his head. The sun did move, for he had seen it, and the earth did not move, for he had been standing on it all the time. "I know what I see," he said triumphantly.

"And I believe Father," said his brother. So mankind divides still—some accepting only what their senses reveal to them, the others believing the Word of God.

Today the term "faith" is more productive of disease than of health. It confuses, misleads, creates alternative skepticism and fanaticism, intellectual resistance and emotional surrender, rejection of genuine religion, and subjection to substitutes. It would be convenient to suggest the word "faith" should be de-emphasized, but that cannot be considering it's important to God, Himself;

Now faith is the substance of things hoped for, the evidence of things not seen. For by it the elders obtained a good report. Through faith we understand that the worlds were framed by the word of God, so that things which are seen were not made of things which do not appear. By faith

Abel offered unto God a more excellent sacrifice than Cain, by which he obtained witness that he was righteous, God testifying of his gifts: and by it he being dead yet speaketh. By faith Enoch was translated that he should not see death; and was not found, because God had translated him: for before his translation he had this testimony, that he pleased God. But without faith it is impossible to please him: for he that cometh to God must believe that he is, and that he is a rewarder of them that diligently seek him (Hebrews 11:1-6).

A powerful tradition also protects it. And there is no substitute for expressing the reality to which the word points. In this book, I will interpret the word, "faith," in a way that will remove the confusing and distorted connotations, some of which come down from generation to generation. I will reveal, to the readers of this book, that it is not some mysterious spiritual quality that one must conjure up. It is not some magical substance that will render our sicknesses and afflictions mute, if we master the skill of "positive confessions." It is not hidden power, within ourselves, that can be mastered that we may use it to acquire wealth. It is, instead, a noun (*pistis* in the Greek) that has its substance and reality in Jesus Christ, our Lord. The Bible describes him as "...the Author and Perfecter of our faith." Because of Him, I can say to you, my brothers and sisters...Faith has come!

Chapter 1

What Faith Is

As you read this book, picture yourself driving through a mile-long tunnel with the electricity not working inside it. At this point, only your headlights can provide the necessary illumination to travel safely. Without them you would travel at the risk of your life or health. As you approach the exit, bright sunlight beckons you. As you leave the tunnel, the natural light renders the light from your headlights useless. You see a sign saying "check your headlights," which reminds you that your car lights are still on. In comparison to the light of day, they are so faint that without this warning you might drain the car's battery needlessly by leaving them on at your next stop.

The church's concept of biblical faith is normally seen from our perspective outside the tunnel—faith is as useless as headlights are in the noon day sun. Faith has been so wrongly defined that we have forgotten the darkness of deception that it was designed by the Creator to guide us through. To most of us traveling in the middle of the darkened mile-long tunnel, description of the blinding light awaiting outside the tunnel of our lives seems unreal. Allow me to challenge your thinking as I provide enlightenment at various points of progression along your spiritual journey. I pray that you be like those that Paul and Silas found at the Berean church.

These were more noble than those in Thessalonica, in that they received the word with all readiness of mind, and searched the scriptures daily, whether those things were so (Acts 17:11).

To challenge your present perceptions on biblical faith, let me ask you three questions now that I will answer as this book unfolds: The first question is, if faith is so essential to our salvation, which it is, why is it omitted from the following commonly used verses in the Word of God to convert sinners?

And brought them out, and said, Sirs, what must I do to be saved? And they said, Believe on the Lord Jesus Christ and thou shalt be saved, and thy house (Acts 16:30-31).

For God so loved the world that he gave his only begotten Son, that whosoever believeth in him should not perish but have everlasting life. For God sent not his Son into the world to condemn the world; but that the world through him might be saved. He that believeth on him is not condemned; but he that believeth not is condemned already, because he hath not believed in the name of the only begotten Son of God (John 3:16-18).

That if thou shalt confess with thy mouth the Lord Jesus and shalt believe in thine heart that God hath raised him from the dead, thou shalt be saved. For with the heart man believeth unto righteousness; and with the mouth confession is made unto salvation (Romans 10:9-10).

The second question is, Why is the word "faith" not used in the entire book of the gospel of John? And the third question is, Why is the word "faith" only recorded twice in the entire Old Testament (Hab 2:4; Deut. 32:20) of the King James Version of the Bible?

If you can answer these questions, you have no need to

hear my recounting the evolution that God took me through that drastically changed my viewpoint on my spiritual journey. If you can't answer these questions, however, then turn on your spiritual headlights, which God has given you in the Person of the Holy Spirit.

As he spake these words, many believed on him. Then said Jesus to those Jews which believed on him, if ye continue in my word, then ye are my disciples indeed; And you shall know the truth, and the truth shall make you free (John 8:30-32).

Howbeit when he, the Spirit of truth, is come, he will guide you into all truth; for he shall not speak of himself; but whatsoever he shall hear, that shall he speak and he will show you things to come. He shall glorify me; for he shall receive of mine, and shall show it unto you (John 16:13-14).

Let me start by defining what faith is; I will also define what faith is not in the next chapter, along with some ramifications.

Faith = *pistis*, noun. It is a confidence that someone or something is reliable. We must have some reliable content to our Christianity. Paul puts the facts of our faith in a nutshell:

For I delivered to you as of first importance what I also received, that Christ died for our sins according to the Scriptures, and that He was buried, and that He was raised on the third day according to the Scriptures, and that He appeared to Cephas, then to the twelve. After that He appeared to more than five hundred brethren at one time, most of whom remain until now, but some have fallen asleep; then He appeared to James, then to all the apostles; and last of all, as it were to one untimely born,

3

He appeared to me also. For I am the least of the apostles, who am not fit to be called an apostle, because I persecuted the church of God (1 Cor. 15:3-9).

Faith can also refer to our body of beliefs as being of "the Christian faith."

But if anyone does not provide for his own, and especially for those of his household, he has denied the faith, and is worse than an unbeliever (1 Timothy 5:8).

Beloved, while I was making every effort to write you about our common salvation, I felt the necessity to write to you appealing that you contend earnestly for the faith which was once for all delivered to the saints (Jude 3).

Believe = *pisteuo*, verb. Many people think that when it states in Acts 16:31, "And they said, 'Believe in the Lord Jesus, and you shall be saved, you and your household...'" it is too easy and simple a method of salvation. Actually, simply believing is very hard for most people. Believing is intellectual in the sense that our faith has to have some facts upon which to rest our minds. We must believe what God says in His Word. But believing also involves deciding for or against Christ and His offer of salvation.

As a verb, *pisteuo* can be used with different prepositions. It is often used with the word "in" *(en)* as in John 3:16, "For God so loved the world that He gave His only begotten Son, that whosoever believes in Him should not perish, but have eternal life." It means to confide in someone or something. It can also be used with the word "on" *(epi,* as in Acts 16:31). This stresses laying hold upon the object of faith.

The use of these prepositions becomes very important when you consider that faith is the means by which the saving work of Jesus is applied to the individual. Salvation comes to the individual when that person places trust in Christ's death

4

on the cross as the complete payment for sin. The combining of these prepositions with "believe" sets up a context that is unique in the New Testament. In other words, the Holy Spirit was communicating through these writers of the Holy Scriptures a new way to accurately describe what "believing" entails.

The gospel writers understood that Jesus was calling men to do more than believe in His existence. They knew something that has been lost to today's casual Christians. From their own experiences, they knew that Jesus Christ was calling on sinners to put their trust in Him, in His life, in His words, and ultimately in His death as payment for their sin.

Sometimes the word "faith" is followed not by a preposition, but by a clause or clauses; Romans 10:8-10,

But what does it say? The word is near you, in your mouth and in your heart that is, the word of faith which we are preaching that if you confess with your mouth Jesus as Lord, and believe in your heart that God raised Him from the dead, you shall be saved; for with the hear man believes, resulting in righteousness, and with the mouth he confesses, resulting in salvation.

To make belief in Christ clearer, since it is the most important step in one's spiritual life, the New Testament uses several terms that are practically synonymous with "believe" when used in the context of faith, such as receive, ask, confess, and call upon. John 1:12 says,

But as many as received Him to them He gave the right to become children of God, even to those who believe in His name.

And John 4:10 states,

5

Jesus answered and said to her, If you knew the gift of God, and who it is who says to you, 'give me a drink,' you would have asked Him and He would have given you living water."

Romans 10:9, "that if you confess with your mouth Jesus as Lord, and believe in your heart that God raised Him from the dead, you shall be saved.

Romans 10:13, "for whoever will call upon the name of the Lord will be saved."

Faithful, Believing = *pistos* (can apply to a believer whether faithful or not). A qualifier for an elder is that his children be pistos. Titus 1:6 says,

namely if any man be above reproach, the husband of one wife, having children who believe, not accused of dissipation or rebellion."

It might ease the minds of many to realize that while some elders have some children who were believers but (at least for a time) not faithful Christians, there is still hope for their transformation. Another translation of pistos is "reliable or trustworthy," especially when it is speaking about a statement made.

This is a trustworthy statement; and concerning these things I want you to speak confidently, so that those who have believed God may be careful to engage in good deeds. These things are good and profitable for men (Titus 3:8).

And He who sits on the throne said, "Behold, I am making all things new." And He said, "Write, for these words are faithful and true" (Rev. 21:5).

In chapter four we will see in more detail how the term "faithful" is related to a believer's eternal security.

Let us now look within the Word of God to see how He defines faith. (We will explore later in this book more applications for our personal use.) The following is the "Hall of Fame" recording in Hebrews 11:1-6 of those whose faith-walk we are to emulate.

Now faith is the substance of things hoped for, the evidence of things not seen. For by it the elders obtained a good report. Through faith we understand that the worlds were framed by the Word of God, so that things which are seen were not made of things which do not appear. By faith Abel offered unto God a more excellent sacrifice than Cain, by which he obtained witness that he was righteous, God testifying of his gifts; and by it he being dead yet speaketh. By faith Enoch was translated that he should not see death; and was not found, because God had translated him; for before his translation he had this testimony, that he pleased God. But without faith it is impossible to please him: for he that cometh to God must believe that he is, and that his a rewarder of them that diligently seek him.

Faith is the means by which we can see the unseen—God. To have faith then is to be persuaded that God exists. Belief is the first evidence of trust. Therefore faith is the confidence in the reliability of God that substantiates things hoped for and is the evidence of things not seen! What is that we hope for? That "blessed hope"—Jesus.

Looking for that blessed hope, and the glorious appearing of the great God and our Savior Jesus Christ; who gave himself for us, that he might redeem us from all iniquity, and purify unto himself a peculiar people, zealous of good works (Titus 2:13-14).

Looking unto Jesus the author and finisher of our faith; who for the joy that was set before him endured the cross, despising the shame, and is set down at the right hand of the throne of God (Hebrews 12:2).

Jesus is our faith! Let us go into His marvelous light. Jesus is our faith! What are the evidences of our faith? In other words, what should we do as a result of our faith? Obey and seek God and His righteousness.

Even so faith, if it has no works, is dead, being by itself (James 2:17).

By this the children of God and the children of the devil are obvious; anyone who does not practice righteousness is not of God, nor the one who does not love his brother (1 John 3:10).

But flee from these things, you man of God; and pursue righteousness, godliness, faith, love, perseverance and gentleness (1 Timothy 6:11).

My little children, I am writing these things to you that you may not sin (1 John 2:1).

Jesus Christ the righteous; All discipline for the moment seems not to be joyful, but sorrowful; yet to those who have been trained by it, afterwards it yields the peaceful fruit of righteousness (Hebrews 12:10-11).

Confidence or Assurance

Faith does not take on a life unto itself, but faith must be in God. No one in Hebrews 11 received anything materially for themselves, for it is not what we want that is important, but what God wants! Often we wish for something rather than have faith about it. If it truly something God wants us to have, we need to have faith that He will bring it to pass and not just wish for it to happen.

The threefold purpose of faith is

1) It gives us access to God.
2) It causes us to be yielded vessels.
3) It gives us assurance of salvation.

For therein is the righteousness of God revealed from faith to faith; as it is written, the just shall live by faith (Romans 1:17).

Wherein ye greatly rejoice, though now for a season, if need be, ye are in heaviness through manifold temptations; that the trial of your faith, being much more precious than of gold that perisheth, though it be tried with fire, might be found unto praise and honor and glory at the appearing of Jesus Christ; whom having not seen, ye love in whom though now though now ye see him not, yet believing, ye rejoice with joy unspeakable and full of glory; receiving the end of your faith, even the salvation of your souls (1 Peter 1:6-9).

Chapter 2

What Faith Is Not

To first understand what faith is not, we only have to remember that faith is a noun, not a verb. As we learned in elementary school, a noun is a person, place, or thing. Christendom today, especially the faith-based prosperity ministry, teach that faith can grow in quantity as we grow spiritually. This is a false assumption that is disputed by the Lord Jesus' teaching. Consider His words:

And when they were come to the multitude, there came to him a certain man, kneeling down to him and saying, Lord have mercy on my son; for he is lunatic, and sore vexed; for oftimes he falleth into the fire, and oft into the water. And I brought him to thy disciples, and they could not cure him. Then Jesus answered and said, O faithless and perverse generation, ho long shall I be with you? How long shall I suffer you? Bring him hither to me. And Jesus rebuked the devil; and he departed out of him, and the child war cured from that very hour. Then came the disciples to Jesus apart, and said, why could not we cast him out? And Jesus said unto them, because of your unbelief; for verily I say unto you, if ye have faith as a grain of mustard seed, ye shall say unto this mountain, remove hence to yonder place; and it shall remove; and nothing shall be impossible unto you. Howbeit this kind goeth not out by prayer and fasting (Matthew 17:14-21).

In this account, Jesus speaks to His disciples who are seeking an answer for their inability to cast out a demon from the son in question. The unasked question is "Were we given the ability to exercise authority over this demon. If so, why did we fail?" Jesus' answer reveals that if faith was an issue of quantity, then even if it was miniscule as a mustard seed, they could still command something as grandiose as a mountain to obey their every whim. The solution to their dilemma was that they needed to pray fervently and fast. The "and fast" was added to this account to reflect the intensity by which they were to depend on the Lord's might and not their own.

Then he answered and spake unto me, saying This is the word of the Lord unto Zerubbabel, saying Not by might, nor by power, but by my spirit saith the Lord of hosts (Zech. 4:6).

Apparently their earlier success had them relying on their own power and not His power.

Confess you faults to one another, and pray one for another, that ye may be healed. The effectual fervent prayer of a righteous man availeth much (James 5:16).

Unfortunately, today many of us have forgotten the following truth.

Now ye are clean through the word which I have spoken unto you. Abide in me and I in you. As the branch cannot bear fruit of itself, except it abide in the vine; no more can ye, except ye abide in me. I am the vine, ye are the branches: He that abideth in me, and I in him, the same bringeth forth much fruit; for without me ye can do nothing (John 15:3-5).

11

This is divine reality. Faith is not ubiquitous or au-
tonomous, nor does it take on life unto itself; faith must be in
God.

> *That is that I may be comforted together with you by the*
> *mutual faith both of you and me. Now I would not have*
> *you ignorant, brethren, that oftentimes I purposed to come*
> *unto you, (but was let hitherto) that I might have some*
> *fruit among you also, even as among other Gentiles. I am*
> *debtor both to the Greeks, and to the Barbarians, both to*
> *the wise and to the unwise. So as much as in me is, I am*
> *ready to preach the gospel to you that are at Rome also.*
> *For I am not ashamed of the gospel of Christ; for it is the*
> *power of God unto salvation to every one that believeth; to*
> *the Jew first, and also to the Greek. For therein is the*
> *righteousness of God revealed from faith to faith; as it is*
> *written; the just shall live by faith* (Romans 1:12-17).

In verse 17, when Paul uses the expression, "faith to faith,"
he is not speaking of faith growing quantitatively, but rather
dispensationally, transitioning from the Old Testament to that
present time. To illustrate, a baby in its mother's womb needs
oxygen to live. However, since the baby cannot breathe on its
own, it lives on its mother's oxygen supply through the umbil-
ical cord. When the child makes its transition from embryo to
infant and the cord is severed, it must begin to breathe life-sus-
taining air on its own. Those created in the image of God are
sustained by what the apostle Paul refers to as a "measure of
faith."

> *For I say, through the grace given unto me, to every man*
> *that is among you, not to think of himself more highly*
> *than he ought to think; but to think soberly, according as*
> *God hath dealt to every man the measure of faith*
> (Romans 12:3).

But unto every one of us is given grace according to the measure of the gift of Christ. Wherefore he saith, when he ascended up on high, he led captivity captive, and gave gifts unto men. (Now that he ascended, what is it but that he also descended first into the lower parts of the earth? He that descended is the same also that ascended up far above all heavens, that he might fill all things.) And he gave some apostles, and some, prophets, and some, evangelists, and some pastors and teachers; for the perfecting of the saints, for the work of the ministry, for the edifying of the body of Christ. Till we all come in the unity of faith, and of the knowledge of the Son of God, unto a perfect man, unto the measure of the stature of the fullness of Christ (Eph. 4:7-13).

Faith Grows in Quality

The change, which Ephesians 4 reflects, clearly shows the spiritual principle that faith grows not in quantity, but quality as our knowledge of the Lord Jesus Christ increases! Our faith grows in quality as we learn of Jesus and trust in His dependability and the viability of His promises. We pray the prayer of faith.

Who are kept by the power of God through faith unto salvation ready to be revealed in the last time. Wherein ye greatly rejoice, though now for a season, if need be, ye are in heaviness through manifold temptations; that the trial of your faith being much more precious than of god that perisheth, though it be tried with fire, might be found unto praise and honor and glory at the appearing of Jesus Christ; Whom having not seen, ye love; in whom though now ye see him not, yet believing, ye rejoice with joy unspeakable and full of glory; receiving the end of your faith, even the salvation of your souls (1 Peter 1:5-9).

The word is nigh thee, even in thy mouth, and in thy heart; that is, the word of faith, which we preach; that if thou shalt confess with they mouth the Lord Jesus, and shalt believe in thine heart that God hath raised him from the dead, thou shalt be saved. For with the heart man believeth unto righteousness; and with the mouth confession is made unto salvation. For the scripture saith, whosoever believeth on him shall not be ashamed. For there is no difference between the Jew and the Greek; for the same Lord over all is rich unto all that call upon him. For whosoever shall call upon the name of the Lord shall be saved. How then shall they call on him in whom they have not believed? And how shall they believe in him of whom they have not heard? And how shall they hear without a preacher? And how shall they preach, except they be sent? As it is written, how beautiful are the feet of them that preach the gospel of peace, and bring glad tidings of good things! But they have not all obeyed the gospel. For Esaias saith, Lord, who hath believed our report? So then faith cometh by hearing, and hearing by the word of God (Romans 10:8-17).

When the "word of faith" is preached and received by receptive ears, the result is that the hearer can believe that Jesus is the Christ.

Adding to Your Faith

You can enhance the quality of your faith by "adding to your faith." How is this done? Let's let Peter explain in II Peter 1:4-6.

Whereby are given unto us exceeding great and precious promises, that by these ye might be partakers of the divine nature, having escaped the corruption that is in the world through lust. And beside this, giving all diligence, add to

*your faith virtue; and to virtue knowledge; and to knowl-
edge temperance, and to temperance patience, and to patience godliness;*

Therefore we, the Body of Christ, must get back to
teaching believers to first "put on Christ." Then the saints can
grow from "faith to faith," enhancing their faith, not in quantity, but quality.

The saints in the Old Testament expressed their belief in
God. Therefore, when, Hebrews 11 says "by faith," it should
say "according to faith," for believing involves deciding for or
against Christ and His offer of salvation. By their believing
God and taking Him at His word, they became a type of Christ
to their contemporaries, thus earning them a place in the Hall
of Faith. They were "looking to Jesus Who was the Author and
Finisher of our faith."

I will expound more on this in the succeeding chapters, but
for now, let me conclude this chapter by saying that the saints
in the Old Testament believed in the promise of God, which
they received by a variety of ways. Therefore, none of them can
be said to have had "faith" as we know it today. For example, it
is said of Abraham, who many call the father of faith, that he
"believed God," not that he had faith in God. The same applies to all other Old Testament heroes. They believed God,
they did not have "faith," as we know it today. Notice that the
writer of Hebrews 1:1-2 says:

*God, who at sundry times and in diverse manners spake
in time past unto the fathers by the prophets, hath in these
last days spoken unto us by his Son, whom he has appointed
heir of all things, by whom also he made the worlds.*

Faith must have "substance" to be real: it must be filled
with content not ideals. It was to come in the New Testament.

Chapter 3

Faith Is In, Works Are Out

S peaking of faith, Andrew Murray says this,

Never try to arouse faith from within. You cannot stir up faith from the depths of your heart. Leave your heart and look into the face of Christ.

John 1:17 says, "For the law was given by Moses, but grace and truth came by Jesus Christ." This verse emphasizes that salvation came about through dispensations. Pertaining to grace, we are also taught in the Word of God that it is through receiving grace through faith, not works, that we obtain our salvation;

> *That in the ages to come he might shew the exceeding riches of his grace in his kindness toward us through Christ Jesus. For by grace are ye saved through faith; and that not of yourselves; it is the gift of God: Not of works, lest any man should boast. For we are his workmanship, created in Christ Jesus unto good works, which God hath before ordained that we should walk in them* (Ephesians 2:7-10).

Therefore faith is in, and works is out! Let me illustrate this in the form of a familiar story. A minister was going to preach. He climbed a hill on the road. Beneath him lay the villages, sleeping in their beauty, with the cornfields motionless in the sunshine. But he did not look at them, for his attention was arrested by a woman standing by her door, and who, upon seeing him, anxiously came over to him.

She asked him, "Oh sir, have you any keys about you? I have broken the keys to my drawers and there are some things I must get directly."

When he said, "I have no keys," she was disappointed, expecting that everyone must have some keys.

"But suppose," he said, "I had some keys; they might not fit your lock and therefore you could still not get the articles you want. Do not distress yourself; wait till someone else shows up. But," said he, wishing to improve the occasion, "have you ever heard of the keys to heaven?"

"Ah yes," she said, "I have lived long enough, and I have gone to church long enough to know that if we work hard and get our bread by the sweat of our brow, act well towards our neighbors, and behave, as the Catechism says, lowly and reverently to our betters, and we do our duty in that station of life in which it has pleased God to place us, and say our prayers regularly, we shall be saved."

"Ah!" said the man, "my good woman, that is a broken key, for you have broken the commandments; you have not fulfilled all your duties. It is a good key, but you have broken it."

"Pray sir," said she, believing that he understood the matter, and looking frightened, "what have I left out?"

"Why," said he, "the all-important thing—the blood of Jesus Christ. Don't you know it is said the key to heaven is His girdle; He openeth and no man shutteth; He shutteth and no man can openeth?" And, explaining it more fully to her, he said, "It is Christ, and Christ alone, that can open heaven to you and not your good works."

"What? Minister," said she, "are our good works useless then?"

"No," said he, "not after faith. If you believe first, you may have as many good works as you please; but if you believe, you will never trust in them; for if you trust in them, you have spoiled them and they are not good works any longer. Have as many good words as you please; still, put your trust wholly in the Lord Jesus Christ; for if you do not, your keys will never unlock heavens gate." James puts it this way:

> *Even so faith, if it hath not works, is dead, being alone. Yea, a man may say, thou hast faith and I have works; shew me thy faith without thy works and I will shew thee my faith by my works. Thou believes that there is one God; thou doest well; the devils also believe and tremble. But wilt thou know, O vain man, that faith without works is dead? Was not Abraham our father justified by works, when he had offered Isaac his son upon the altar? Seest thou how faith wrought with his words and by works was faith made perfect? And the scripture was fulfilled which saith, Abraham believed God and it was imputed unto him for righteousness; and he was called the Friend of God. Ye see then how that by works a man is justified, and not by faith only. Likewise also was not Rahab the harlot justified by works when she had received the messengers and had sent them out another way? For as the body without the spirit is dead, so faith without works is dead also* (James 2:17-26).

Notice the dispensational concept that James is expounding on; it is consistent with John's words that we had looked at earlier, and it is in line with the apostle Paul's words in his epistles.

Concerning the dispensation of faith, there are four principles that must be learned:
1) The basis of salvation is the death of Jesus Christ.
2) The requirement of salvation is faith.
3) The object of faith is the true God.
4) The content of faith changes in the various
   dispensations.

The evolution of faith from a noun to a verb in the theology of many in Christendom has its roots in modern eschatology. It has its roots in the movement away from the church's earlier dealing with the problem of evil in the world by offering a theodicy (a vindication of God's justice). Today, many have replaced sound theology about faith with one of hope. Instead of asking why God does not do something about evil in the world, the latter school acts to transform that evil. To them faith has become an action word, which, in turn, will help to bring about the object of that faith. In reality, it is an emotional movement that feeds off the material longings of the American dream. It wins converts by promising to break the chains of necessity that bind us. Thus, it promise to change us from wimps and ordinary little people into nothing less than "little gods."

The truth is that Jesus calls us to follow Him in the way of the cross, where the delivering signs and wonders, so promoted in today's charismatic ministries, do not always happen. In fact, the troubles that we pray to be freed from can become the material out of which God fashions the saints into becoming overcomers;

These things I have spoken unto you, that in me ye might have peace. In the world ye shall have tribulation; but be of good cheer; I have overcome the world (John 16:33).

The word "overcome" does not mean the absence from

19

trouble, but it is synonymous with surmounting and prevailing over, as well as to overwhelm. Very relevant to this is the saying of C.S. Lewis, "Miracles are for beginners." When we are in the early stages of the Christian life, where we are "adding to our faith," as He is confirming who He is and building us up, God will often show Himself to be the rescuer, who gets us out of our trouble. When, however, we become stronger and more mature, He will give us the opportunity to honor Him, not by delivering us, but by calling us to follow Jesus through the dark, even deadly places where no relief comes, to the new life that lies on the other side.

What heals us are not esoteric techniques or even special supernatural endowments; what heals us is the love we witness at Calvary. The key to wholeness is not speaking in tongues or the healing of our memories, but in thanking God for everything with emphasis that "His will be done." It is Calvary's love that drives out the demons from our lives. It is the word of the Suffering Servant who bears our sins, shares our sufferings, and cures our diseases. He does this as we identify with Him and accept His moving ever further into His costly identification with us, taking on Himself what is destroying us, penetrating His love into the very heart of what is wrong with us, and so sharing His own wholeness with us. As Paul puts it in Romans 5:5,

> *And hope maketh not ashamed; because the love of God is shed abroad in our hearts by the Holy Ghost which is given unto us.*

The reason that there is so little healing and renewal in our midst is not because of the absence of the charismatic gifts, but it is rather an absence of this quality of love (see 2 Cor. 13).

Dispensationalism

Another school of eschatology, of which I belong, is dispensationalism. It is the interpretive scheme that is advocated in most conservative circles. Dispensationalism is a unified interpretive system. That is to say, each part or tenet is vitally interconnected with the others. It is a method of interpreting Scripture.

Dispensationalists find in God's Word evidence of a series of "dispensations" or economies under which God has managed the world. It has manifested in successive stages in the unfolding of the revelations of God's plan or purposes. They do not entail a different means of salvation, for the means of salvation has always been the same in all periods of time, namely, by grace through faith in Jesus Christ.

The most common perception is that there have been seven dispensations, although this is by no means verifiable. As this belief goes, man was first in the dispensation of innocence. Then came the dispensation of conscience (from the fall to the flood), human government (from the flood to the call of Abraham), then consecutively promise, law, and grace. In the eye of the dispensationalist's thinking, the seventh is yet to come. (For more information on dispensationalism see *Dispensationalism Today* by Charles C. Ryrie, there he contrasts the differing views of dispensationalism, as what distinguishes it from the other theological schools of thought.)

The emphasis of this book is that while it is extremely relevant to the Christian that "without faith it is impossible to please God," we must not change the biblical meaning to appease our conscience. We must remember that while we are saved by "grace through faith," Ephesians 2:8-9 must be seen in the proper context:

> *For by grace are ye saved through faith; and that not of yourselves; it is the gift of God; not of works, lest any man should boast.*

The phrase, "...it is the gift of God," identifies faith as the

"the gift," and grace is the source of that gift, namely, Jesus Christ (see John 1:17). That is why having faith, in itself, is not a meritorious act. When that faith is manifested in believing then it can be said that we are "born again." Like the baby that is birthed from its mother's womb and breathes on its own, we now have the presence of the Holy Spirit in us to help us live the Christian life. The permanence of this Person of the Trinity, in us, sets us apart from our counterparts in the Old Testament. Thus, we grow "out of faith" (before the incarnation of Jesus), "into faith" (after the birth of Jesus). (See Romans 1:17, 12:3).

> *Jesus answered and said unto him, verily, verily, I say unto thee, except a man be born again, he cannot see the kingdom of God. Nicodemus saith unto him, how can a man be born when he is old? Can he enter the second time into his mother's womb and be born? Jesus answered, verily, verily I say unto thee, except a man be born of water and of the Spirit, he cannot enter into the kingdom of God. That which is born of the flesh is flesh; and that which is born of the Spirit is spirit. Marvel not that I said unto thee, ye must be born again* (John 3:3-7).

Nevertheless, the *content* of faith has changed through the various dispensations. Faith is still defined as the confidence in the reliability of God. In its essence, it is the substantiating of "things hoped for and the evidence of things not seen" (Hebrews 11:1). Faith is not a verb or action word to bring about the object of faith. Instead, the object of faith is the true God in the manifested incarnation of His Son. Faith came not by the action of man. Faith came by way of various dispensations, in the Person of Jesus Christ;

> *God, who at sundry times and in diverse manners spake in time past unto the fathers by the prophets, hath in these*

last days spoken unto us by his Son, whom he hath ap-
pointed heir of all things, by whom also he made the
worlds; who being the brightness of his glory, and the ex-
press image of his person, and upholding all things by the
word of his power, when he had by himself purged our sins,
sat down on the right hand of the Majesty on high
(Hebrews 1:-3).

Have you said of yourself that you are "born again?" Then understand that the phrase "from faith to faith" is synonymous with the born again experience. The chief goal of man should be to please God, and in doing so, we please ourselves. For we then activate inner joy, which gives substance to our temporal and eternal welfare. Man cannot please God without bringing to himself a great amount of happiness. If any man pleases God, it is because God accepts him as a son, gives him the blessings of adoption, pours upon him the bounties of His grace, and makes him a blessed man in this life. It insures him a crown of everlasting life which he shall wear and which will shine with unachromatized glowing, when the wreaths of earth's glory have all melted away.

On the other hand, if a man does not please God, he inevitably brings upon himself sorrow and suffering in this life. Furthermore, he puts a worm and rottenness in the core of his life. He fills his death pillow with man-made thorns, and he supplies the eternal fire with embers of flames which shall forever consume him. Common sense rejects the latter path and beckons us to follow the former trajectory, for His divine grace will lead us onward unto the ultimate reward of all those who love and fear Him, who are "born again," and who have grown from "faith to faith." Therefore, strive earnestly as you can, live excellently as you please, make what sacrifices you choose, be as eminent as you can for everything that is lovely and of good repute, yet understand, that none of these things, of themselves, can be pleasing to God unless they are mixed with faith.

Or as the Lord said about the Hebrew children in Leviticus 2:13,

> *And every oblation of thy meat offering shalt thou season with salt; neither shalt thou suffer the salt of the covenant of thy God to be lacking from thy meat offering; with all thine offerings thou shalt offer salt.*

When He says to them, "with all your sacrifices you must offer salt," He says to us that have traversed from faith to faith. "With all your actions or offerings you must bring faith, for without the gift of faith it is impossible to please Him. He is such a good God that all He ever asks us to give to Him is what He first gives to us!

Faith comes...and when it comes, we need to return to Him that gives it by living lives directed by it!

Chapter 4

The Gospel Plan for Sinful Man

We are guilty of "sin" and "sins." But God has a plan of salvation for us. The simple plan of salvation is:

- Our guilt has earned us the death penalty.
- Jesus Christ died in our place.
- We must admit that we are guilty.
- We must have "faith" in the atoning work of our Savior.
- We must "believe" that Jesus was punished in our place.
- If we accept Jesus as our Lord and Savior we are declared "not guilty" by the Almighty God.

That's it! The simple plan of salvation. John refers to it as gaining "eternal life" and becoming "children of God." Paul prefers the term "justification".

Therefore being justified by faith, we have peace with God through our Lord Jesus Christ; by whom also we have access by faith into this grace wherein we stand, and rejoice in the glory of God (Romans 5:1-2).

What shall we say then that Abraham our father, as pertaining to the flesh, hath found? For if Abraham were justified by works, he hath whereof to glory; but not before God. For what saith the scripture? Abraham believed God, and it was counted unto him for righteousness. Now to him that worketh is the reward not reckoned of grace, but of debt. But to him that worketh not, but believeth on him that justifieth the ungodly, his faith is counted for righteousness (Romans 4:1-5).

To declare, I say, at this time his righteousness; that he might be just, as the justifier of him which believeth in Jesus (Romans 3:26).

Clearly, Paul declares that our heavenly Father has pronounced "not guilty"on those who qualify. And yet many struggle with the fear of losing their salvation. But how can we lose Christ's payment for our sin? Can God declare us guilty after He has already declared us not guilty?He can't and still remain true to His Word.

That by two immutable things, in which it was impossible for God to lie, we might have a strong consolation, who have fled for refuge to lay hold upon the hope set before us (Hebrews 6:18).

God is not a man, that he should lie; neither the son of man, that he should repent; hath he said, and shall he not do it? Or hath he spoken, and shall he not make it good? (Numbers 23:19)

If you question your salvation, then you do not have faith that Jesus Christ died for your sin, resulting from descending from Adam (Romans 5:12,19) and "sins," resulting from your personal disobedience. If you have a problem with the thought that a child of God can be eternally secure, then you have a distorted understanding of what happened on the cross. This can be stated categorically: When there is uncertainty concerning how salvation is attained, there will be confusion whether it can be maintained.

The simple truth is that salvation has always been by faith alone! This element of faith is a gift from God, placed in us by Him, which must be cultivated by the individual. True enough, there is a measure of faith in every man (Romans 12:3). However, "saving" faith is a gift of God that transforms us from guilty to guiltless. Therefore, we are no longer under condemnation. This is the "free gift" that the apostle Paul spoke of in Romans 5:15-16,

> But not as the offense so also is the free gift. For if through the offense of one many be dead, much more the grace of God and the gift by grace, which is by one man, Jesus Christ, hath abounded unto many. And not as it was by one that sinned, so is the gift; for the judgment was by one to condemnation, but the free gift is of many offenses unto justification.

The combination of our inherent sinfulness and our ensuing acts of sin puts us in bad standing before God, but we are not condemned (v. 16). On the contrary, we are "declared righteous."

Without faith in Jesus we would face the inevitability of being separated from God as it says in Romans 6:23, "For the wages of sin in death; but the gift of God is eternal life through Jesus Christ our Lord." We are all included in Romans 3:23, "For all have sinned and come short of the glory of God."

The latter two verses say a lot about the consequences of sin. Why is the concept of eternal security of the believer important? Because everyone will live forever, somewhere, and when the Bible speaks of death it does not mean annihilation. Death means separation. In this instance, it means separation from God.

Romans 6:23 tells the consequences facing all sinner and

Romans 3:23 tells us why this must occur. Even before we commit "sins," our "sin" makes us ineligible for the perfection needed to dwell forever with God who is holy and pure. His nature demands that we be guiltless, for His nature determines the standard for those who desire a relationship with Him.

This is not some arbitrary set of rules that God established to make it difficult for us. If that were so, Christ died in vain. No! God's high standard flows from His immutable nature. Child of God, there are changes that must be made: changes that we are hopelessly incapable of making ourselves. Guilt must be irradiated, or to put it another way, salvation at its core is the removal of guilt, both personal and imputed.

Now the problem. How can a perfect God make a guilty person not guilty? The simple answer is "by faith." However, since all saints do not feel this security, this simple answer needs clarification. Dr. Charles Ryrie says in his book, Basic Theology, (pp. 298-299).

> There are only three options open to God as sinners stand in His courtroom, He must condemn them, compromise His own righteousness to receive them just the way they are, or He can change them into righteous people. If He can exercise the third option, then He can announce them righteous, which is justification.

The apostle Paul makes it clear that Christians have been justified, and there is no conflict between God's justice and His willingness to justify sinners (Romans 5:1). Furthermore, Paul settles the issue by saying in II Corinthians 5:21,

> *For he hath made him to be sin for us, who knew no sin, that we might be made the righteousness of God in him."*

Charles Stanley, in his book, *Eternal Security*, describes it this way; "God made a swap...He imputed our sin to Christ and His righteousness to us." The swap was that our sin was exchanged for His righteousness and vice versa. However, in doing so, Jesus suffered being separated from God (death). Remarkably, though He was separated from God for our sake, yet He is now sitting at the right hand of God, interceding for us.

Now of the things which we have spoken this is the sum: We have such a high priest, who is set on the right hand of the throne of the Majesty in the heavens; A minister of the sanctuary, and of the true tabernacle, which the Lord pitched, and not man (Hebrews 8:1-2).

How could this be? Dr. Stanley responded to this apparent dilemma by saying, "As Christ hung on the cross, God abandoned Him. The separation was so real that Christ even addressed God differently."

And when the sixth hour was come, there was darkness over the whole land until the ninth hour. And at the ninth hour, Jesus cried with a loud voice saying, Eloi, Eloi, Iama sabachthani? Which is being interpreted, My God, my God, why has thou forsaken me? (Mark 15:33-34)

"Until that time" says Dr. Stanley, "He had referred to God as His Father. Suddenly, however, the fellowship was broken and Jesus shouted out not 'My Father' but 'My God!' The intimacy was gone. Christ was alone."

The penalty of our sin was paid in full. The punishment was death, physically and spiritually. What enabled fellowship to be restored? It was Jesus' own righteousness. As the Christ, He had committed no sin, nor did He have sin nature.

Hereafter I will not talk much with you; for the prince of this world cometh, and hath nothing in me (John 14:30).

Therefore, there was nothing to keep Jesus Christ from reuniting with the Father after a brief period of separation. The sinlessness of the Lamb of God made Him the only acceptable sacrifice for sin. If Jesus died for one of our sins, He died for all of them;

> *For the law having a shadow of good things to come, and not the very image of the things, can never with those sacrifices which they offered year by year continually make the comers thereunto perfect. For then would they not have ceased to be offered? Because that the worshippers once purged should have had not more conscience of sins. But in those sacrifices there is a remembrance again made of sins every year. For it is not possible that the blood of bulls and goats should take away sins. Wherefore, when he cometh into the world, he saith, sacrifice and offering thou wouldest not, but a body hast thou prepared me; in burnt offerings and sacrifices for sin thou hast had no pleasure. Then said I, lo, I come (in the volume of the book it is written of me) to do thy will, O God. Above when he said, sacrifice and offering and burnt offerings and offering for sin thou wouldest not, neither hadst pleasure therein; which are offered by the law; Then said he, Lo, I come to do thy will, O God. He taketh away the first that he may establish the second. By which will we are sanctified through the offering of the body of Jesus Christ once for all. And every priest standeth daily ministering and offering oftentimes the same sacrifices, which can never take away sins; But this man, after he had offered on sacrifice for sins for ever, sat down on the right hand of God; from henceforth expecting till his enemies be made his footstool. For by one offering he hath perfected for ever them that are sanctified* (Hebrews 10:1-14).

How can anyone undo all that? If Christ took upon Himself every single one of our sins, what is going to cause God to go back on His word? He declared the believer "not guilty." The answer is no one or nothing. We are adopted into the family of God forever. We cannot be unadopted. Praise God! We are adopted forever. Not only that, we are sealed by the Holy Spirit.

Labor not for the meat which perisheth, but for that meat which endureth unto everlasting life, which the Son of man shall give unto you; for him hath God the Father sealed. And I give unto them eternal life and they shall never perish; neither shall any man pluck them out of my hand. My Father, which gave them me, is greater than all; and no man is able to pluck them out of my Father's hand. I and my Father are one (John 6:27-30).

Now he which establisheth us with you in Christ, and hath anointed us, is God; Who hath also sealed us, and given us the earnest of the Sprit in our hearts (II Corinthians 1:21-22).

In whom ye also trusted, after that ye heard the word of truth, the gospel of your salvation; in whom also after that ye believed, ye were sealed with that Holy Spirit of promise (Ephesians 1:13).

Scripture teaches that regardless of the consistency of our faith, our salvation is secure. This truth is taught both by proposition and illustration. Paul sums it up this way,

It is a faithful saying; For if we be dead with him, we shall also live with him; If we suffer, we shall also reign with him; if we deny him, he also will deny us; If we believe not, yet he abideth faithful; he cannot deny himself (II Timothy 2:11-13).

If we are faithless, He remains faithful! There are four theological truths that substantiate this truth given to Timothy by the aging apostle.

First we are co-crucified with Jesus our Lord.

I am crucified with Christ; nevertheless I live; yet not, I but Christ liveth in me; and the life which I now live in the flesh I live by the faith of the Son of God, who loved me, and gave himself for me (Galatians 2:20).

The second reason is directly related to our suffering;

If we suffer, we shall also reign with him; if we deny him, he also will deny us (II Timothy 2:12).

And the reality is recorded in II Timothy 3:12,

Yea and all that will live godly in Christ Jesus shall suffer persecution.

The third reason comes from the words of Jesus as recorded in Matthew 10:32-33,

Whosoever therefore shall confess me before men, him will I confess also before my Father which is in heaven. But whosoever shall deny me before men, him will I also deny before my Father which is in heaven.

However, the fourth reason, as stated to comfort Timothy, is that even if a believer loses or abandons their faith they will retain their salvation because Jesus remains faithful for He cannot deny Himself. He is our faith! Our faith came when He appears!

Faithful is he that calleth you, who also will do it (1 Thess. 5:24).

Chapter 5

By Faith We Are Eternally Secure

For I am not ashamed of the gospel of Christ; for it is the power of God unto salvation to every one that believeth; to the Jew first, and also to the Greek. For therein is the righteousness of God revealed from faith to faith; as it is written, the just shall live by faith (Romans 1:16-17).

Why should we be ashamed of a Gospel that pronounces us "not guilty?" We don't have to apologize for a message that says we are "saved by grace through faith." After all, God does not ask men to behave, but to believe. It is faith in Christ that saves the sinner, and eternal life in Jesus the Christ is one gift that is for everyone regardless of their need or their situation in life. For it is not exclusive to national origin or gender. Salvation is the great need of the human race. The former Pharisee declares to a Roman people who are obsessed with power, that he can proclaim to them a power greater than their emperor's that can heal in ways unknown to their physicians. There is a city that the philosopher Seneca called "a cesspool of iniquity." Paul offers a solution. He promised personal and national deliverance if they would heed his message. The testimony he gives as proof is the same one that we can give today—it changed his life. The apostle means that he glories in the gospel and counts it a high honor to proclaim it.

"For in it," Paul says, "the righteousness of God is revealed." This divine attribute intrinsically reveals both God's personal righteousness and that righteousness needed to justify sinners through faith. It is based on faith and addresses faith (faith to faith). It starts with faith and ends in faith. It extends from the faith of God revealing, to the faith of man receiving, from a faith of dependence upon God (Old Testament) to a faith that depends on a Mediator, and from a faith that introduces us into a justified state, to one by which we live our lives for. "...the just shall live by faith."

What distinguishes the faith that was exhibited in the first dispensations from the one present during the dispensation of grace is that we are the only ones that can say positively we are possessors of eternal security. There are presently two schools of thought on the doctrine of eternal security. The first view falls within the framework of the Armenian theology. This view believes that a born-again believer can lose his salvation by turning away from or no longer believing or trusting in Jesus Christ. They refer to this kind of person as an apostate. The classic passage they use for proof of their belief is Hebrews 6:4-6,

> *For it is impossible for those who were once enlightened, and have tasted of the heavenly gift, and were made partakers of the Holy Ghost. And they have tasted the good word of God, and the powers of the world to come. If they shall fall away to renew them again unto repentance; seeing they crucify to themselves the Son of God afresh, and put him to an open shame.*

Let's look close at those verses in Hebrews because many commentators avoid it or bypass it altogether. I take the position that the ones that Paul is referring to here are the Jewish believers of the first century, and the warning applies only to them. At the time this epistle was written, the temple was still standing, and the apostle was warning the Jewish Christians about returning to the sacrificial system, because in doing so they would be admitting that Jesus did not die for their sins. However, as far as the word "impossible" goes, the reality is that while it is impossible for man, it is possible for God.

Then said Jesus unto disciples, verily I say unto you, that a rich man shall hardly enter into the kingdom of heaven. And again I say unto you, it is easier for a camel to go through the eye of a needle than for a rich man to enter into the kingdom of God. When his disciples heard it, they were exceedingly amazed saying, who then can be saved? But Jesus beheld them, and said unto them. With them this is impossible; but with God all things are possible (Matthew 19:23-26).

The main issue for proponents of the opposite view is faithfulness, resulting in a person turning away from the church, Christ, and all that He stands for. It is a deliberate stepping out of this kingdom of light into the realm of darkness. They argue that man, as a free moral agent, has the freedom to renounce his previous choice for Christ and choose to deny Him. They also refer to the words "fallen," "fallen away," or "depart" as Scriptural proof relating to "the faith" as in, I Timothy 4:1-7,

Now the Spirit speaketh expressly, that in the latter times some shall depart from the faith, giving head to seducing spirits, and doctrines of devils; speaking lies in hypocrisy; having their conscience seared with a hot iron....

Christ is become of no effect unto you, whosoever of you are justified by the law; ye are fallen from grace, for we through the Spirit wait for the hope of righteousness by faith. For in Jesus Christ neither circumcision availeth any thing nor uncircumcision, but faith which worketh by love. Ye did run well; who did hinder you that ye should not obey the truth? (Galatians 5:4-7)

As the principle goes, it is impossible for any man to enter heaven on our own; we have a Savior, thank God, a Redeemer. Of Himself, He says:

Jesus saith unto him, I am they way, the truth, and the life; no man cometh unto the Father but by me (John 14:6).

Paul then qualifies this by speaking directly to the church when he says:

But, beloved we are persuaded better things of you, and things that accompany salvation, though we thus speak (Hebrews 6:9)..

He says that the issues relevant to the church is not about, to quote J. Vernon McGee, "the fruit of salvation, but the root of salvation." In other words, Paul is speaking of the fruit of the Christian life and the subsequent reward that follows it. However, I differ with Mr. McGee when I state that the eternal security relating to salvation is germane only to those saved during the dispensation of grace.

The other view is the Calvinist view, which is expressed as "once saved always saved." It maintains that once you are saved, you can never be lost. They explain away any contradictions presented by one in their midst that is revealed to be lost by saying that they were never really saved at all. Among their strongest biblical arguments are:

And I give unto them eternal life; and they shall never perish, neither shall any man pluck them out of my hand. My Father, which gave them me, is greater than all; and no man is able to pluck them out of my Father's hand (John 10:28-29).

All that the Father giveth me shall come to me; and him that cometh to me I will in on wise cast out (John 6:37).

My position, I repeat, is that there is a doctrine of eternal security, but it is relevant only to those who are fortunate to live during the age of grace; thus, the significance of the phrase, "faith came." Let us examine Paul's words given to the Galatian Church;

But before faith came, we were kept under the law, shut up unto the faith which should afterwards be revealed. Wherefore the law was our schoolmaster to bring us unto Christ, that we might be justified by faith. But after that faith is come, we are no longer under a schoolmaster, for ye are all the children of God by faith in Christ Jesus (Gal. 3:23-26).

This closing section of Galatians 3 follows Paul's teaching regarding the true purpose of the law. This is contingent on a change taking place, and this change justifies our new standing before God. Paul has just taught that the true purpose of the law is to lead men to Christ. Now, though he began with this point, he soon moved on to the idea of a change of position for those who have passed from being under the bondage of the law, as under a schoolmaster. We are sons, having been reconciled to God and made one with another by way of the baptism of the Holy Spirit.

For as the body is one, and hath many members, and all the members of that one body, being many are one body, so also is Christ. For one Spirit are we all baptized into one body, whether we be Jews or Gentiles, whether we be bond or free; and have been all made to drink into one Spirit (I Cor. 12:12-13).

The proper understanding of the phrase, "before this faith came," is found in the fact that the word "this" occurs before the word "faith." Frank E. Gaebelein says in *The Expositor's Bible Commentary*, Vol. 10,

It is true that Paul can refer to faith generically as that on which every successful approach to God is founded. But this is not his meaning here. By "this faith" he means "the Christian faith," that faith he has just spoken of in v.22—faith in Jesus Christ as Savior.

This faith is somewhat the same thing spoken about in the faith exercise of Abraham. The only difference is that it relates to the explicit revelation of Christ in time and to the distinct Christian doctrines concerning Him. Faith waited for this complete revelation. Paul's point is that the law was intended to function only during this 1,500 year period of anticipation.

> *But the scripture hath concluded all under sin, that the promise by faith of Jesus Christ might be given to them that believe* (Galatians 3:22).

This verse, as well as the succeeding verses, refers to the law as confining or locking up man under the law. Why? In order that by faith we might be justified (v. 24). However, it is the new status as "children of God by faith" that we acquire that which allows us to be secure. Why? Paul puts it this way:

> *But after that faith is come, we are no longer under a schoolmaster, for ye are all the children of God by faith in Christ Jesus. For as many of you as have been baptized into Christ have put on Christ* (Galatians 3:25-27).

Being children of God can only be said of those who are baptized into the Body of Christ by the Holy Spirit. This is why faith is not mentioned in relation to anyone in the Old Testament. The lives of the Old Testament saints are not characterized by the definition of the word "faith."

This is hard stuff. I pray though that you are not ready to accuse God of being unfair to those of the previous dispensation. The reality is that God is not fair, but He is just. We must not challenge the authority of God to be partial to His children. The real issue is not one of uncertainty or diplomacy, but one of sonship.

> *But we see Jesus, who was made a little lower than the angels for the suffering of death, crowned with glory and honor; that he by the grace of God should taste death for every man. For it became him, for whom are all things, and by whom are all things in bringing many sons unto glory, to make the captain of their salvation are all of one; for which cause he is not ashamed to call them brethren. Saying, I will declare thy name unto my brethren, in the midst of the church will I sing praise unto thee* (Hebrews 2:9-12).

It is for this reason that "faith came" in the Person of Jesus (Hebrews 12:2). Let us look at one of Jesus' parables to see if this unique relationship applies.

> *But what think ye? A certain man had two sons; and he came to the first and said, son, go work today in my vineyard. He answered and said, I will not; but afterward he repented and went. And he came to the second, and said likewise. And he answered and said, I go, sir; and went not. Whether of them twain did the will of his father? They say unto him, the first. Jesus saith unto them, verily I say unto you, that the publicans and the harlots go into the kingdom of God before you. For John came unto you in the way of righteousness, and ye believed him not; but the publicans and the harlots believed him; and ye, when ye had seen it, repented not afterward, that ye might believe him* (Matthew 26:28-32).

Here in Matthew's Gospel, after the Son of Man responded to the chief priests and elders together, the scribes of the Sanhedrin publicly challenged His authority to make Messianic claims (Matthew 21:23-27).

He spoke three parables to them, beginning with the one that preceded this paragraph.

This parable emphasizes that what counts with God is not promise but performance. Though the attitude of the leaders toward the tax collectors and the harlots [who these officials despised and regarded us as furthest from pleasing God (see Matthew 9:9-10)] stands out, in reality, these elitists are the ones excluded from the presence of God. The wording, "...go into the kingdom of God before you," does not explicitly include or exclude the religious leaders from the kingdom of God. The contrasting attitudes of the sons in the parable suggest that the verb points to the precedence of one over the other. This slant is even more apparent later on in this chapter;

They say unto him, He will miserably destroy those wicked men, and will let out his vineyard unto other husbandmen, which shall render him the fruits in their seasons. Jesus saith unto them, did ye never read in the scriptures, the stone which the builders rejected, the same is become the head of the corner, this is the Lord's doing and it is marvelous in our eyes? Therefore say I unto you, the kingdom of God shall be taken from you and given to a nation bringing forth the fruits thereof (Matthew 21:41-43).

The leaders' failure was not merely due to a lack of moral and religious sincerity, but rather in the fact that they had failed to recognize and welcome God's saving action in the ministry of His Son, as the outcasts had clearly done. These religious leaders could not recognize the way of righteousness.

Counsel is mine and sound wisdom: I am understanding; I have strength. By me kings reign and princes degree justice. By me princes rule and nobles, even all the judges of the earth. I love them that love me; and those that seek me early shall find me. Riches and honor are with me; yea, durable riches and righteousness. My fruit is better than gold, yea, than fine gold and my revenue than choice silver. I lead in the way of righteousness, in the midst of the paths of judgment; That I may cause those that love me to inherit substance; and I will fill their treasures. The Lord possessed me in the beginning of his way, before his works of old. I was set up from everlasting, from the beginning, or ever the earth was (Proverbs 8:14-23).

Jesus taught righteousness both through His life and in His teaching. By aligning Himself to John the Baptist, Jesus was saying that if they had believed John, they would have believed Him. The solemn pronouncement in verse 43, "Therefore I say unto you..." suggests that there is a new people of God in place of Old Testament Israel. This "transfer" is not to the Gentiles, in general, but to a people of God that is composed of both Jew and Gentile. They are now the "holy nation."

But ye are a chosen generation, a royal priesthood, a holy nation, a peculiar people; that ye should show forth the praises of him who hath called you out of darkness into his marvelous light (I Peter 2:9)

As a result of the dispensational change, there is both continuity and discontinuity. The reign of God continues, but the composition of that "nation" is changed by a new principle that recognizes those who produce fruits and not solely on those with a particular ethnic background.

Most biblical scholars have no problem believing that Scripture teaches about God's promises that the Church has a heavenly destiny, while Israel's destiny involves the "holy land." My contention is that only those who have been privileged to have lived during or after the Lord uttered the words from the cross, "It is finished," can be the benefactors of the doctrine of eternal security. Only they can say "faith has come." Only they can be called "adopted sons and daughters."

Chapter 6

By Faith We Are Sealed

In the once bloody battlefield at Saratoga there stands a towering obelisk—a 155-foot high monument commemorating the decisive struggle where the British made their last stand over two centuries ago. In the distance are the stately Adirondack and Taconic mountains. It is a solemn and sober moment when visitors stand on that windswept hill, savoring a slice of national history. The monument gives mute testimony to those heroes of yesteryear who refused to bow the knee to England.

About its base are four niches, and in each niche appear the name of one of the commanding American generals. Above the names stand giant bronze figures on horseback, as famous today as in the day they shouted their orders. You can almost hear the voices of Horatio Gates, Philip John Schuyler, and Daniel Morgan.

But the niche on the fourth side is strangely vacant. The name appears, but the soldier is absent. As we read the name, our minds rush on to the foggy banks of the Hudson where the man sold his soul and forfeited the right to be remembered. The name is that of the brigadier general who once commanded West Point and distinguished himself in battles along Lake Champlain, Mohawk Valley, Quebec, and Saratoga but who committed treason and died—the infamous Benedict Arnold. As Clarence McCartney once put it so eloquently, "The empty niche in that monument shall ever stand for fallen manhood, power prostituted, for genius soiled, for faithlessness to a sacred trust."

The man who turned traitor despised the Puritan morality of his mother and died in greater disgrace and poverty than his drunken father. There is another empty niche, far more famous and in sharp contrast to that monument in the state of New York. It too stands in memory of a battle, but not the kind fought with guns and bayonets. This niche is actually an empty tomb, a place that once held a body, in fact, the most significant body that ever housed a human soul. The tomb was borrowed and "used" for only a short time, but in perfect fulfillment of Scripture, it enveloped the dead Messiah.

The battle against sin had been bloody and treacherous. Anyone who had the courage to visit the tomb shortly after it was sealed would certainly have wept bitterly. The battlefield, strewn with the litter of an awful fight, was only too vivid in everyone's memory—a small pile of clothing, a spear, a matted network of thorns in the shape that would fit around a head, and a bloody cross. And those words, those final words the victim uttered still hung in the air, especially that awful scream—"*Eloi, Eloi, lama sabachthani!*"

But what appeared to be defeat was actually the preface of victory. The ugly, rugged cross took its toll, but it failed to have the final voice.

Deep in the silence of night, against all odds and in the mockery of strong-armed soldiers, the Victim became the Victor. "Up from the grave He arose, with a mighty triumph over His foes," or as Charles Wesley wrote of that Easter morning miracle:

Love's redeeming work is done, Alleluia!
Fought the fight, the battle won, Alleluia!

Death in vain forbids Him rise, Alleluia!
Christ has opened Paradise, Alleluia!

The bloody battlefield paled into a misty memory as the tomb opened its jaws for all to enter. Death could not keep its prey...He tore the bars away...He came back from beyond.

The above illustration was taken from the pages of Charles R. Swindoll's book entitled, *Come Before Winter...And Share My Hope*. How many Christians have lost the hope of their salvation? How many have questioned the ability of God to keep them because they had been defeated by the enemy? How many Benedict Arnolds are there in our midst? How many "empty niches" are in our congregations because people are living lives that are synonymous with disgrace when they should be present and singing "How Great Thou Art"? Why? Because they have not really grasped what happened on the Cross at Calvary, they not only question their salvation, but they are downtrodden because they do not have the "faith to move mountains." (I will return to teaching about biblical faith, but for now I will focus on the doctrine of eternal security.) This is biblically correct; everyone who has been saved has been sealed by the Holy Spirit and they can proclaim as Paul did:

For which cause I also suffer these things; nevertheless I am not ashamed for I know whom I have believed and am persuaded that his is able to keep that which I have committed unto him against that day (II Timothy 1:12).

Being confident of this very thing that He which hath begun a good work in you will perform in until the day of Jesus Christ (Phil. 1:6).

Imagine opening a newly purchased jar of food. Think of the assurance we get as to the freshness of the product when we hear the breaking of the seal. The resulting "pop" gives us confidence that the jar has not been tampered with. In the same way, there is a "seal" that assures each believer that no one has interfered with our security that we have in Jesus Christ;

In whom ye also trusted, after that ye heard the word of truth, the gospel of your salvation; in whom also after that ye believed, ye were sealed with that Holy Spirit of promise, which is the earnest of our inheritance until the redemption of the purchased possession, unto the praise of his glory (Ephesians 1:13-14).

The sealing that the apostle is referring to belongs only to those who are possessors of the Holy Spirit. This sealing carries with it the idea of protection and security. It is a promise that God gives exclusively to those that are "established in Christ" and "by faith ye stand," or as Paul wrote to the church at Corinth,

For all the promises of God in him are yea, and in him Amen, unto the glory of God by us. Now he which establisheth you in Christ, and hath anointed us is God; who hath also sealed us and given the earnest of the Spirit in our hearts. Moreover I call God for a record upon my soul that to spare you I came not as yet unto Corinth. Not for that we have dominion over your faith, but are helpers of your joy; for by faith ye stand (I Cor. 1:20-24).

To those who teach that we exist in the never-never land of salvation—sometimes we are there and at other times we are not there. I challenge everyone to answer this question: What significance would a seal have if it could be continually removed and reapplied? What does it really seal?

Were the saints in the previous dispensations sealed? Yes.

Was that sealing permanent? In some instances. Consider this picture in the book of Revelation,

> *And I heard the number of them which were sealed; and there were sealed a hundred and forty and four thousand of all the tribes of the children of Israel. Of the tribe of Judah were sealed twelve thousand. Of the tribe of Reuben were sealed twelve thousand. Of the tribe of Gad were sealed twelve thousand. Of the tribe of Aser were sealed twelve thousand. Of the tribe of Nepthalim were sealed twelve thousand. Of the tribe of Manassas were sealed twelve thousand. Of the tribe of Simeon were sealed twelve thousand. Of the tribe of Levi were sealed twelve thousand. Of the tribe of Issachar were sealed twelve thousand. Of the tribe of Zabulon were sealed twelve thousand. Of the tribe of Joseph were sealed twelve thousand. Of the tribe of Benjamin were sealed twelve thousand* (Revelation 4:4-8).

We can see the permanence of their seals because this entire group reappears later on in this book:

> *And I looked and lo a Lamb stood on the mount Sion, and with him a hundred forty and four thousand, having his Father's name written on their foreheads. And I heard a voice from heaven, as the voice of many waters, and as the voice of a great thunder; and I heard the voice of harpers harping with their harps; and they sun as it were a new song before the throne, and before the four beasts and the elders and no man could learn that song but the hundred and forty and four thousand, which were redeemed from the earth. These are they which were not defiled with women; for they are virgins. These are they which follow the Lamb whithersoever he goeth. These were redeemed from among men, being the first fruits unto*

God and to the Lamb. And in their mouth was found no guile; for they are without fault before the throne of God (Revelation 14:1-5).

However, unlike the seals on the 144,000—their seal was some sort of mark in their forehead—our seal is not visible. Nevertheless, it protected them during the most dangerous time. Not even the Antichrist could break the seals.

Comparatively speaking, the seals spoken of by Paul are spiritual. During the age of grace we are given the Holy Spirit as a pledge of God's intent to save us. With that promise is the reality that the Holy Spirit is not finished with us—our roofs are not on yet. This "Comforter" demonstrated God's commitment to "complete what He has begun" (Phil. 1:6). Just as the 144,000 who bore His seal were safe, we are too. No spiritual or physical force can break our seal.

And grieve not the holy Spirit of God, whereby ye are sealed unto the day of redemption (Ephesians 4:30).

And not only they, but ourselves also which have the first fruits of the Spirit, even we ourselves groan with ourselves, waiting for the adoption to wit, the redemption of our body (Romans 8:23).

Praise God, everyone who is spiritually sealed will remain sealed.

Who are kept by the power of God faith unto salvation ready to be revealed in the last time (I Peter 1:5).

We are protected by the Almighty God! However, the argument of the apostle Paul, in Galatians 3:-4:20, is that salvation by grace is the only assurance that a guilty sinner can be saved by a holy God. In fact, he says that if a member that has been saved by grace reverts back to dependence on the law, he is not saved. The problem is not His law, for it is good. It reflects His divine attributes and tells us that He wants us to stay within the boundaries He has set. The problem exists because knowing the law and believing it to be a revelation of God's standard does not prevent us from breaking it. As Paul says in Romans Chapter 7, the law demonstrated our complete inability to earn our salvation, and it prepares us to receive the message of grace. That is the only doorway that leads to eternal fellowship with God.

The question is; could a person who was saved before "faith came," lose their salvation? I believe they could based on the strength of Paul's warning in Galatians 1:6-9.

> *I marvel that ye are so soon removed from him that called you into the grace of Christ unto another gospel, which is not another, but there be some trouble with you, and would pervert the gospel of Christ. But though we or an angel from heaven, preach any other gospel unto you than that which we have preached unto you, let him be accursed. As we said before, so I say now again. If any man preach any other gospel unto you than that ye have received, let him be accursed."*

Clearly Paul is giving a strong warning to the Galatians not to "pervert" the gospel of Jesus Christ. Among his warning were that they could be "accursed." Obviously being cursed by God is inconsistent with being saved by the Holy One. Consider, that Paul says of himself in Galatians 1:10,

> *For do I now persuade men or God? Or do I seek to please men? For if I yet pleased me, I should not be the servant of Christ.*

In the latter verse of this chapter, he says that if he became a man pleaser, then he would not be a "servant of Christ." I conclude that if Paul could call into question his calling, then he is also calling into question the salvation of the offending members of this church. This is consistent with his words to the Hebrews:

> *For it is impossible for those who were once enlightened, and have tasted of the heavenly gift and were made partakers of the Holy Ghost. And have tasted the good word of God and the powers of the world to come. If they shall fall away, to renew them again unto repentance; seeing they crucify to themselves the Son of God afresh, and put him to an open shame* (Hebrews 6:4-6).

You may argue that these individuals did not "lose" their salvation. However, it is clear that they were not saved. Instead, they were influenced by Judaizers who did not believe that the gospel message was sufficient to save a soul, of itself. They insisted that to be saved you had to keep the law as well. Therefore, they "perverted" the Gospel, and they were to suffer the punishment reserved for the damned.

This Pauline epistle teaches that law and grace cannot co-exist in one's life and keep you in good standing before God. These Old Testament legalists did not deny the facts of the Gospel, but they misinterpreted those facts. By doing so, they were saying that the blood of Jesus was not sufficient to save us by itself. This is one of the oldest heresies known, and it is still present today. In his warning to these Galatian "believers," Jesus dies once for all sins, and He will not die again.

> *By which will we are sanctified through the offering of the body of Jesus Christ once for all. And every priest standeth daily ministering and offering oftentimes the same sacrifices, which can never take away sins. But this man, after he had offered one sacrifice for sins for ever, sat down on the right hand of God. From henceforth expecting till his enemies he made his footstool. For by one offering he hath perfected for ever them that are sanctified* (Hebrews 10:10-14).

For if we sin willfully after that we have received the knowledge of the truth, there remaineth no more sacrifice for sins (Hebrews 10:26).

Can the law bring life? No! No more than a fall from a high skyscraper brings life to one who fell from its roof. Likewise, "but before faith came, we were kept under the law, shut up onto the faith which should afterwards be revealed." Here Paul is speaking of faith in Jesus. The reward for possessors of that faith is the "sealing."

The apostle Paul's demonizing of the place and purpose of the law was necessary to spare the saints a terrible plight. The reason he classifies us all as sinners and allows us to see the justification for his strong language is that we may be eligible for salvation. After all, Jesus said the "righteous" have no claim on Christ; it was for "sinners" that He came (Matthew 9:12-13). Seen from this angle, even the condemnatory function of the law is all of grace; and this is what Paul has already insisted in the latter half of Galatians 3:22 and expands upon his meaning in the succeeding 4 verses.

"Before (Christian) faith came," we were held under arrest by the law awaiting the divine revelation of the faith that was to come. Seen in this light, the law was our "escort" to lead us to our Lord Jesus so that we might be justified by trust. We can now say of God, "Abba Father," for we are now His children by way of adoption.

Chapter 7

By Faith We Are Adopted

Since the function of the law was essentially preparatory, it could not make a child into a "son." According to the Jewish tradition, there had to be a ceremonial rite directed by the father to initiate the transition from childhood to full sonship. Using Paul's human analogy, faith in Christ has given us full sonship to God. Law still has its place in the life of a Christian, but it is the law of love—the law of Christ.

Bear ye one another's burdens, and so fulfill the law of Christ (Galatians 6:2).

From God's perspective, the failure of the law is that it couldn't give a child the nature required of a son of God. Only faith in Christ can make us sons of God. It is important to make this distinction. It is not faith plus something that equals salvation, but *faith plus nothing* makes you a son of God. Consider that an individual Hebrew, under the law in the Old Testament dispensations, was never a son, only a servant. It is true, however, that the nation of Israel was called a son, but never an individual Hebrew.

And thou shalt say unto Pharaoh, Thus saith the Lord, Israel is my son, even my firstborn (Exodus 4:22).

On the other hand, Moses, the speaker of the verse above,

was intimate with God and was referred to as a "servant of Jehovah." For example,

> *Now after the death of Moses the servant of the Lord it*
> *came to pass that the Lord spoke unto Joshua the son of*
> *Nun, Moses' minister saying, Moses my servant is dead;*
> *now therefore arise, go over this Jordan, thou and all this*
> *people, unto the land which I do give to them, even to the*
> *children of Israel* (Joshua 1:1-2)..

This was his epitaph. Likewise, David was a "man after God's own heart"; nevertheless, God calls him "David, My servant" (I Kings 11:38), and not My son.

After being born "from above" through the ennoblement of the Holy Spirit, it can only be said of one saved during the present age,

> *But as many as received him, to them gave he power to be-*
> *come the sons of God, even to them that believe on his*
> *name* (John 1:12).

We are given the power, authority, and the right to become the sons of God only after it could be said that "faith came." We can attain this status simply by trusting the One referred to as coming, preceding the "Hall of Fame of Faith" in Hebrews 11.

> *Cast not away therefore your confidence, which hat great*
> *recompense of reward. For ye have need of patience, that*
> *after ye had done the will of God ye might receive the*
> *promise. For yet a little while and he that shall come will*
> *come, and will not tarry. Now the just shall live by faith;*
> *but if any man draw back my soul shall have no pleasure*
> *in him. But we are not of them who draw back unto*
> *perdition; but of them that believe to the saving of the soul*
> (Hebrews 10:35-39).

Justification, or the state that is referred to in verse 38

above, has a negotiational connotation to it. Consider that when a judge pronounces a man "not guilty," it does not necessitate a change in the nature of the magistrate's relationship with the one receiving judgment. The jurist can be hostile or apathetic to the sentence because he gains or loses nothing personally. Thanks be to God we are not only acquitted, but we are forgiven. We are not only released from the obligation to pay for our sins, but because Jesus died for our sins, we are forgiven. Because He has forgiven us, when we accept Jesus as our Lord and Savior, we are adopted as sons by the Father. Additionally, we can have fellowship with Him because of our new bond.

The difference between an earthly judge and our heavenly One is reflected in the relationship we can have with each. The apostle Paul chose something from their culture and their nature that would best illustrate this unique relationship between a holy God and a fallen man. The Holy Spirit directed the apostle to use the term "adoption" to portray more accurately this process by which God establishes an alliance with the person who believes that Jesus is the Christ.

Notice how Paul emphasizes the relational value of adoption in Romans 8:15-16,

> *For ye have not received the spirit of bondage again to fear; but ye have received the spirit of adoption, whereby we cry, Abba, Father. The Spirit itself beareth witness with our spirit, that we are children of God.*

In these verses we are prompted to think about our heavenly Father in the most intimate way, as a daddy. This relationship is contrasted to one based on fear, as between a judge and the accused or a slave and its master. It denotes the intimate fellowship of a father with his child. This intimacy is echoed in Galatians 4:4-5 as well,

But when the fullness of the time was come, God sent for His Son, made of a woman, made under the law. To redeem them who were under the law, that we might receive the adoption of sons.

Paul connects the principles of adoption and justification. Our justification was merely a means to an end. God's ultimate goal was always to bring about a truly intimate relationship between man and Himself. Justification was simply a necessary step in God's ultimate plan of restoration.

In the Old Testament dispensation, God is always pictured as a Judge, never a Father. However, during the age of grace, God has walked from behind the bench to welcome us into His family. This is also seen in John 5:24,

Verily, verily, I say unto you, He that heareth my word and believeth on him that sent me hath everlasting life, and shall not come into condemnation; but is passed from death unto life.

As believers today, we will never be judged for our sins. The death of Jesus settled that issue in the mind of God. The question is no longer will God accept us into His family, but will we take comfort in our new standing. If salvation wasn't permanent, why would God introduce the concept of adoption? He could have just described salvation in terms of a conditional legal contract between God and man. Again, the reality is that this was His plan from the beginning, as demonstrated in Ephesians 1:3-14,

Blessed be the God and Father of our Lord Jesus Christ, who hath blessed us with all spiritual blessings in heavenly places in Christ; according as he hath chosen us in him before the foundation of the world, that we should be holy and without blame before him in love; having predestinated us unto the adoption of children by Jesus Christ to himself according to the good pleasure of his will, to the praise of the glory of his grace, wherein he hath made us accepted in the beloved. In whom we have redemption through his blood, the forgiveness of sins, according to the riches of his grace; wherein he hath abounded toward us in all wisdom and prudence; having made known unto us the mystery of his will, according to his good pleasure which he hath purposed in himself; that in the dispensation of the fullness of times he might gather together in one all things in Christ, both which are in heaven, and which are on earth; even in him. In whom also we have obtained an inheritance, being predestinated according to the purpose of him who worketh all things after the counsel of his own will. That we should be to the praise of his glory, who first trusted in Christ. In whom ye also trusted, after that ye heard the word of truth, the gospel of your salvation; in whom also after that ye believed, ye were sealed with that Holy Spirit of promise, which is the earnest of our inheritance until the redemption of the purchased possession, unto the praise of his glory.

God chose to adopt us as His children before the foundation of the world! That is a biblical certainty. Why then is it so rarely referred to by theologians? Possibly because they have not seen its dispensational connection. Let me share with you what Dr. Herbert Lockyear says, in his book, *All the Doctrines of the Bible,*

Much can be gathered on regeneration, but its twin truth of adoption is dispensed with. Should it be? It is not a definite part of the whole counsel of God? Prime aspects of a divine revelation are connected with adoption.

Apparently puzzled, Dr. Lockyear reasons that,

It may be that this theme is neglected because of the fact that a believer is a son of God through the work of the Holy Spirit. Being born then into the family of God, how can he be adopted when cooptation means the entrance into a family of one unrelated? What is the explanation of the Biblical fact that the saints, made sons by the new birth, are also treated as adopted ones? Prayerfully seeking the tuition of Him who is the Spirit of adoption…

As I try to fill in the missing blanks, I repeat that the answer is both the failure of the Old Covenant to change the heart of a sinful man, and need for such a change to truly transform the sons of men into the sons of God. Faith is the key. God only adopts those into His family who have been born again. Scripturally speaking, adoption implies a change of nature as well as a change of relationship. That is why after "faith came," then and only then could God do what He promised in Jer. 31:31-34,

> *Behold, the days come, saith the Lord, that I will make a new covenant with the house of Israel, and with the house of Judah. Not according to the covenant that I made with their fathers in the day that I took them by the hand to bring them out of the land of Egypt; which my covenant they brake, although I was a husband unto them, saith the Lord. But this shall be the covenant that I will make with the house of Israel; after those days saith the Lord, I will put my law in their inward parts, and write it in their hearts; and will be their God and they shall be my people. And they shall teach no more every man his neighbor, and every man his brother, saying, know the Lord for they shall all know me, from the least of them unto the greatest of them, saith the Lord, for I will forgive their iniquity, and I will remember their sin no more.*

Sonship must precede adoption. Those born again by the Holy Spirit and adopted by God experience the impartation of the divine nature. As His Spirit enter them, those who are God's by faith in Jesus Christ receive not only His love and grace but His disposition as well. A filial disposition can only come in a filial relationship. Through the new birth, the believer effectively acquires spiritual disposition and character. The idea of adoption can be compared to the process of grafting that Paul refers to in Romans 11. Of Israel, Paul teaches that the branches (Israel) "were broken off" that the Gentiles might "be grafted in" (Romans 11:19). Paul uses stern words to explain the spiritual principle that the rejected Israel reveals the judgment reserved for those who reject Jesus. Thankfully we can receive the grace of the Father if we believe on His Son by faith. He puts it this way in Romans 11:21-24,

> *For if God spared not the natural branches, take heed lest he also spare not thee. Behold therefore the goodness and severity of God; on them which fell, severity, but toward thee, goodness, if thou continue in his goodness; otherwise thou also shalt be cut off. And they also, if they abide not still in unbelief, shall be grafted in; for God is able to graft them in again. For if thou wert cut out of the olive tree which is wild by nature, and were grafted contrary to nature into a good olive tree; how much more shall these, which be the natural branches be grafted into their own olive tree?*

These two sides of God are also revealed in His granting only to those baptized into the *ecclesia* (Church) the assurance of their salvation. According to the apostle's words, the restoration of Israel will come after they are, in turn, grafted into the church.

> *And I will pour upon the house of David, and upon the*

*inhabitants of Jerusalem, the spirit of grace and of suppli-
cations; and they shall look upon me whom they have
pierced, and they shall mourn for him, as one mourneth
for his only son, and shall be in bitterness for him, as one
that is in bitterness for his firstborn* (Zech. 12:10).

Nevertheless, the way in which we become sons shows that
sonship is peculiar to this dispensation (Gal. 3:26). Not only
are the adopted ones called sons today, but they are also called
children and heirs. "Children" refers to our nearness to the
Father; "sons" expresses our position before Him; "heirs"
speaks of our future inheritance in Him. By comparison, Old
Testament saints were called children but not sons. Sonship is
reserved for those who possess the eternal character that is cultivated in them during the age of grace.

*He that overcometh shall inherit all things; and I will be
his God, and he will be my son* (Rev. 21:7).

*But is under tutors and governors until the time ap-
pointed of the father. Even so we, when we were children,
were in bondage under the elements of the world; But
when the fullness of the time was come, God sent forth his
Son, made of a woman, made under the law. To redeem
them that were under the law, that we might receive the
adoption of sons* (Gal. 4:2-5).

On the other hand, angels are spoken of as "sons," but not
children. They lack a filial relationship with God because they
lack the birth-tie that we are privileged to have. However, it
was not without a steep price being paid. This "sonship" is dependent upon the cross and upon the ascension of the One
who shed His blood on that cross for our sins. Therefore,
thanks to Jesus, we who are, otherwise, heirs of wrath, become
heirs of the promise because "faith came."

Because Jesus is the essence of our faith, we have a glorious inheritance as children (Rom. 8:17), and our positions as sons are assured. A wonderful future awaits us! Furthermore, adoption is also to end in our coronation into the kingdom of God and we are made His children and joint heirs with His only begotten Son. Therefore, because we belong to His family, we must uphold the reputation and honor of our "Daddy." All because "faith has come."

Chapter 8

The Way and Walk of Faith

But without faith it is impossible to please him; for he that cometh to God must believeth that he is and that he is a rewarder of them that diligently seek him (Hebrews 11:6).

The reality of the verse above is that it maintains that there has never been a recorded case in the Scriptures of a man, which pleased God, that did not exhibit faith. The 11th chapter of Hebrews is the chapter that lists men and women who pleased God. Notice the recurring theme.

By faith Abel offered unto God a more excellent sacrifice than Cain, by which he obtained witness that he was righteous, God testifying of his gifts; and by it he being dead yet speaketh. By faith Enoch was translated that he should not see death; and was not found, because God had translated him; for before his translation he had this testimony that he pleased God. By faith Noah, being warned of God of things not seen as yet, moved with fear, prepared an ark to the saving of his house; by which he condemned the world and became heir of the righteousness which is by faith. By faith Abraham, when he was called to out into a place which he should after receive for an inheritance,

60

obeyed; and he went out, not knowing whither he went. By faith he sojourned in the land of promise, as in a strange country, dwelling in tabernacles with Isaac and Jacob, the heirs with him of the same promise; for he looked for a city which hath foundations, whose builder and maker is God. Through faith also Sara herself received strength to conceive seed, and was delivered of a child when she was past age, because she judged him faithful who had promised. Therefore sprang there even of one, and him as good as dead, so many as the stars of the sky in multitude and as the sand which is by the sea shore innumerable. These all died in faith, not having received the promises, but having seen them afar off, and were persuaded of them, and embraced them, and confessed that they were strangers and pilgrims on the earth. For they that say such things declare plainly that they seek a country. And truly, if they had been mindful of that country from whence they came out, they might have had opportunity to have returned. But now they desire a better country, that is, a heavenly; wherefore God is not ashamed to be called their God; for he hath prepared for them a city. By faith Abraham, when he was tried, offered up Isaac; and he that had received the promises offered up his only begotten son, of whom it was said, that in Isaac thy seed be called; accounting that God was able to raise him up, even from the dead; from whence also he received him in a figure. By faith Isaac blessed Jacob and Esau concerning things to come. By faith Jacob, when he was dying, blessed both the sons of Joseph; and worshipped, leaning upon the top of his staff. By faith Joseph, when he died made mention of the departing of the children of Israel and gave commandment concerning his bones. By faith Moses, when he was born, was hid three months of his parents, because they saw he was a proper child; and they were not afraid of the king's commandment. By faith Moses, when he was come to years, refused to be called the son of Pharaoh's daughter; Choosing rather to suffer affliction with the people of God, than to enjoy the pleasures of sin for a season; esteeming the reproach of Christ greater riches than the treasures in Egypt; for he had respect unto the recompense of the reward. By faith he forsook Egypt, not fearing the wrath of the king; for he endured, as seeing him who is invisible. Through faith he kept the Passover, and the sprinkling of blood, lest he that destroyed the first-born should touch them. By faith they passed through the Red Sea as by dry land; which the Egyptians assaying to do were drowned. By faith the walls of Jericho fell down, after they were compassed about seven days. By faith the harlot Rahab perished not with them that believed not, when she had received the spies with peace. And what shall I more say? For the time would fail me to tell of Gideon, and of Barak, and of Samson, and of Jephthae; of David also, and Samuel, and of the prophets; who through faith subdued kingdoms, wrought righteousness, obtained promises, stopped the mouths of lions. Quenched the violence of fire, escaped the edge of the sword, out of weakness were made strong, waxed valiant in fight, turned to flight the armies of the aliens. Women received their dead raised to life again; and others were tortured, not accepting deliverance; that they might obtain a better resurrection; and others had trial of cruel mocking and scourging, yea, moreover of bonds and imprisonment; they were stoned, they were sawn asunder, were tempted, were slain with the sword; they wandered about in sheepskins and goatskins; being destitute, afflicted, tormented. (Of whom the world was not worthy) they wandered in deserts, and in mountains, and in dens and caves of the earth. And these all, having obtained a good report

*through faith, received not the promise. God having pro-
vided some better things for us, that they without us should
not be made perfect* (Hebrews 11:4-40).

There have been others mentioned on the pages of
Scripture that have done commendable deeds, but God did not
accept their efforts. Men have humbled themselves, such as
Ahab, but God did not forgive them. Men have repented, such
as Judas, and yet God did not save them. Men have confessed
their sins, such as King Saul, and they continued as they did
before. Multitudes have confessed the name of Christ, as many
modern pastors could testify, but they were not converted.
Why? They did not have faith! The Hebrews 11 covers over
4,000 years of human history. If there was not one person
other than those listed above worthy enough to be mentioned,
then we must ask—what is God telling us about faith? It tells
us that the list covers six dispensations—innocence, conscience,
human government, promise, law, and grace.

Another fact we see evident in the lives of those mentioned
is that they were not too proud to stoop down before God.
Without faith there is no "stooping" grace. Unless man stoops,
his sacrifice cannot be accepted. Without faith, man is more
likely to respond as Cain did rather than as Abel did. Whereas
Cain would not yield his intellect, obey God in a childlike
manner, or believe God's commands willingly. He was too
proud! Faith tells us that we must go to Christ on bent knees;
for though He is a door big enough that one can enter in while
erect, humility requires that we stoop to enter His passageway.
There never was a man who could walk into salvation erect!

*But we are all as an unclean thing, and all our right-
eousness are as flighty rags; and we all do fade as a leaf;
and our iniquities, like the wind, have taken us away*
(Isaiah 64:6).

Consequently, Jesus said,

*...I am the way, the truth, and the life, no man cometh
unto the Father but by me* (John 14:6).

The 11th chapter of Hebrews is distinguished from all
other chapters in the Bible because of its emphasis on faith. It
links the heroes of old specifically with their acts of faith. The
term "by faith" is attached to the deed of these previous generations. However, faith is a present reality and is not the exclusive property of these dynamic men and women. For example,
even today, faith gives us convictions about creation. Look at
Hebrews 11:3,

*Through faith we understand that the worlds wee framed
by the word of God, so that things which are seen were not
made of things which do appear.*

It tells us that "through faith," we agree with Genesis 1
that the world was formed by the words of God and not by any
preexistent material. Therefore, faith requires that we are
single-minded in our belief that creation originated from God.
As the writer puts it, the visible did not originate from the visible; the universe does not account for itself. Faith assures us
that it came from God.

The author of Hebrews then gives a dispensational slant as
he tells of those whose faith pleased God. He begins by
looking to remote antiquity and showing through the lives of
Abel and Enoch the way of faith (Abel), and walk of faith
(Enoch), during the dispensations of innocence and conscience
respectfully.

The Way of Faith

Scripture tells us that Abel brought God a more acceptable
sacrifice than did his brother Cain (Gen. 4:3-7). Why was
Abel's sacrifice superior? Was it because Abel's sacrifice was

living or that it grew spontaneously? The answer is no! Scripture never says that there was anything inherently superior in Abel's offering. While I believe that it is relevant that Abel was a righteous man (Matthew 23:35; 1 John 3:12), Hebrews says that his offering was a demonstration of his faith. Through him, God set forth the way of faith—that men must approach Him only one basis, "by faith." Abel's sacrifice to God stands as a witness that the "more excellent" sacrifice of Abel was for expiatory reasons and not Eucharistic ones. The main point is that Abel is not to be thought of as one long since dead and of no consequence today. He is dead, but his faith is still living. Notice that Abel's blood cried out for vengeance and it was heard by God. See the connection to Jesus' blood crying out for mercy in Hebrews 12:24,

> *And to Jesus, the mediator of the new covenant, and to the blood of sprinkling, that speaketh better things than that of Abel.*

However, Abel's blood couldn't atone for sins, only Jesus Christ's blood is efficacious (I John 1:7). Abel's life does, in fact, reflect the way of faith in a fourfold sequence:
1) He was the first one of the human race to die.
2) He was the first person on the earth to be murdered.
3) He was the first man to be associated with Christ.
4) He was the first saint to present an acceptable
   sacrifice to God.

Though his loss of life does not come close to the efficacy of Jesus' blood that was shed in order to save all humanity, it is resonant on the pages of Scripture as man's first attempt to please God by an act of faith.

The Walk of Faith

And Enoch lived sixty and five years, and begat

Methuselah. And Enoch walked with God after he begat Methuselah three hundred years, and begat sons and daughters. And all the days of Enoch were three hundred sixty and five years. And Enoch walked with God and he was not, for God took him (Genesis 5:21-24).

Enoch's life was characterized by four things:
1) His holy life on earth.
2) His glorious exit from the earth.
3) He "walked with God" by faith.
4) He is the only one spoken of as responding to God according to faith during this dispensation.

Through Enoch, God shows that once man comes into the knowledge of the truth by faith, he can forsake his environment and follow his Creator. The seventh man from Adam was a descendent of the aforementioned Cain, and yet he enjoyed close communion with God. Surprisingly, there is nothing suggestive of God or service to God in the record of his father, Lamech, or any of his close family members. Quite the contrary, his family members mark the growing voluptuousness and luxury of the day. It was a time of transition to art and refinement, replete with the accompaniment of the evils they can bring forth. Consider Enoch's environment: Lamech was the first to have two wives! (Genesis 4:19). Adah, his wife's name, means adornment, pleasure, the decorated. At that time women were beginning to be fashion conscious and were inclining toward pleasure. Adah's sons were (1) Jabal, who was a cattleman. Men began to profit through business enterprises. (2) Jubal, who was the father of musical instruments. Men were beginning to enjoy music and amusement. Lamech's other wife was Zillah, which means shadow of darkness, and she bore Tubal-cain, who became the founder of ancient crafts of metal smiths and iron-makers. Yet, Enoch's character and conduct was a distinct rebuke to a godless world.

Jude says of him in verses 14-15,

And Enoch also, the seventh from Adam, prophesied of these saying, behold the Lord cometh with ten thousands of his saints. To execute judgment upon all and to convince all that are ungodly among them of all their ungodly deeds which they have ungodly committed, and of all their hard speeches which ungodly sinners have spoken against him.

How did God turn Enoch to Himself? He warned him of the coming judgment. When he was 65 years old, Methuselah was born. Through the naming of his son (Methuselah means "it [deluge] shall be sent"), it can be assumed that God had revealed to him of the coming judgment by way of the flood.

Enoch's "walking with God" implies progress in that he did not walk with God for a while and then stop; each day found him actively striving with God. So much so that God says in Hebrews 11:5-6 that He was pleased with this man

By faith Enoch was translated that he should not see death; and was not found; because God has translated him; for before his translation he had this testimony, that he pleased God. But without faith, it is impossible to please him; for he that cometh to God must believe that he is, and that he is a rewarder of them that diligently seek him.

How was Enoch translated to heaven? By faith! He was rewarded for being true to the Word of God. It should encourage us today that if we walk with God, we will also be rewarded. As with Enoch, we must not only start well, but we must end well. Upon what must our faith be based? Paul puts it this way in I Corinthians 15:1-4,

Moreover, brethren, I declare unto you the gospel which I preached unto you, which also ye have received, and

wherein ye stand; by which also ye are saved, if ye keep in memory what I preached unto you, unless ye have believed in vain. For I delivered unto you first of all that which I also received, how that Christ died for our sins according to the scriptures; and that he was buried, and that he rose again the third day according to the scriptures.

Enoch is the only one of his line of whom it could not be said that "he died." That the Scriptures say that "he was not" suggests that his friends and family looked for him. By walking in faith, we too have hope that we will escape coming God's judgment.

Verily I say unto you, this generation shall not pass away till all be fulfilled. Heaven and earth shall pass away; but my words shall not pass away. And take heed to yourselves, lest at any time your hearts be overcharged with surfeiting, and drunkenness, and cares of this life and so that day come upon you unawares. For as a snare shall it come on all them that dwell on the face of the whole earth? Watch ye therefore, and pray always that ye may be accounted worthy to escape all these things that shall come to pass, and to stand before the Son of man (Luke 21:32-36).

But I would not have you to be ignorant, brethren, concerning them which are asleep, that ye sorrow not, even as others which have no hope. For if we believe that Jesus died and rose again, even so them also which sleep in Jesus will God bring with him. For this we say unto you by the word of the Lord, that we which are alive and remain unto the coming of the Lord shall not prevent them which are asleep. For the Lord himself shall descend from heaven with a shout, with the voice of the archangel, and with the trump of God; and the dead in Christ shall rise first; then we which are alive and remain shall be caught up to-

*gether with them in the clouds, to meet the Lord in the
air; and so shall we ever be with the Lord. Wherefore comfort one another with these words* (I Thess. 4:13-18).

What we can learn from Enoch's life about how faith determines who is eligible to be raptured out of this world at this
second coming of Jesus Christ? First, each of us must walk with
the Lord until we too receive the witness that we please God.
Then, we too will be raptured by "faith." Although every believer will be raptured eventually, however, the first to be raptured will be those whose walk of faith deems them worthy to
be noted as overcomers and spared the Tribulation experience:

> *For from you sounded out the word of the Lord not only in
> Macedonia and Achaia, but also in every place your faith
> to God-ward is spread abroad; so that we need not to
> speak any thing. For they themselves shew of us what
> manner of entering in we had unto you, and how ye
> turned to God from idols to serve the living and true God;
> and to wait for his Son from heaven, whom he raised from
> the dead, even Jesus, which delivered us from the wrath to
> come* (1 Thess. 1:8-10).

If you do not walk by faith, as Enoch did, I do not believe
you will be raptured prior to the coming judgment of God.
You may not walk with God as Enoch did for 300 years.
However, your faith must be the motivation behind your believing in the rapture. May God give us all faith to believe.

One factor that set Enoch's walk apart from other men is
that he walked in good conscience with God. We can learn
from him that faith and conscience are connected. The reality
is that when your conscience is breached, your faith is destroyed also. Know this, your faith can be damaged if your conscience is compromised, and without faith there will be no
rapture. Many believers do not believe in the rapture because

they do not walk with God. If we walk day by day with the Lord, like Enoch, our faith will increase in quality, and we will believe that we too will be "delivered from the wrath to come." Enoch believed that he would be rewarded. Let us walk before God with a good conscience, waiting single-mindedly for the coming rapture. As we believe in God, let us also pray for deliverance. Today is our time of preparation that when we arrive in heaven, we will not feel strange in the Lord's presence because we have constantly talked to Him in our lifetime. If Enoch could do it, is there any reason that we can't? After all…"faith has come."

Chapter 9

The Witness of Faith

For whatsoever is born of God overcometh the world; and this is the victory that overcometh the world, even our faith. Who is he that overcometh the world, but he that believeth that Jesus is the Son of God? (I John 5:4-5)

bel's life reflects the way of faith, and Enoch's life illustrates the walk of faith. Faith is the anchor needed to "please God." However, at the beginning of the second dispensation, the question must be asked, what is needed in a world that doesn't please God? The answer is that we need the witness of faith! Enter Noah; of him the Bible says in Hebrews 11:7,

> *By faith Noah, being warned of God of things not see as yet, moved with fear, prepared an ark to the saving of his house; by which he condemned the world, and become heir of the righteousness which is by faith.*

The dispensation of government was initiated after the Lord God acted in judgment as he prophesied through Enoch. The flood brought about the end of the human race, save one family. "By faith Noah...to the saving of his house." Many of us laugh at the fact that Noah preached 120 years and never made a convert. In reality, that is not true. He won his family, and in doing so he kicked off a new dimension in the area of witnessing. Of course, his "faith" led him to believe God when the Lord told him that He would destroy the earth by flood. Then, for 120 years he labored to build an ark to the exact specification set forth by God. Through his life he showed that a life directed by faith in God will always stand in condemnation of wickedness.

> *The men of Ninevah shall rise in judgment with this generation, and shall condemn it; because they repented at the preaching of Jonas; and, behold a greater than Jonas is here. The queen of the south shall rise up in the judgment with this generation and shall condemn it; for she came from the uttermost parts of the earth to hear the wisdom of Solomon; and behold a greater than Solomon is here* (Matthew 12:41-42).

> *The queen of the south shall rise up in the judgment with the men of this generation, and condemn them; for she came from the utmost parts of the earth to hear the wisdom of Solomon; and behold, a greater than Solomon is here. The men of Nineveh shall rise up in the judgment with this generation, and shall condemn it; for they repented at the preaching of Jonas; and behold a greater than Jonas is here* (Luke 11:31-32).

> *Not as Cain, who was of that wicked one, and slew his brother. And wherefore slew he him? Because of his own works were evil, and his brother's righteous* (I John 3:12).

"By faith" Noah stood alone. He was the only person mentioned in the Word that lived during the dispensation of government who is said to have expressed faith in God. The wickedness of his generation is set forth clearly in Genesis 6:5-8,

> *And God was that the wickedness of man was great in the*

earth, and that every imagination of the thoughts of his heart was only evil continually. And it repented the Lord that he had made man on the earth, and it grieved him at his heart. And the Lord said I will destroy man whom I have created from the face of the earth; both man and beast, and the creeping thing, and the fowls of the air; for it repententh me that I have made them. But Noah found grace in the eyes of the Lord.

Surely this was a bad time in the history of mankind. However, there was one godly man that came to the rescue of his generation;

These are the generations of Noah; Noah was a just man and perfect in his generations, and Noah walked with God (Genesis 6:9).

Now listen to J. Vernon McGee words, "Does this mean he was only a nice man who paid his debts and did many helpful things for people? No, he did more than that: Noah walked with God." How did he walk with God? The writer of Hebrews tells us; "by faith…" Noah built an ark. Why? Because God told him!

Just as Jesus hammered home their guilt to His generation by drawing comparison to a previous generation of the queen of Sheba, Noah's generation stood convicted by the witness of the one that they teased—Noah. They did not respond to the words of Noah. Why? It takes faith for one to respond affirmatively to God! Likewise, today's generation will stand before God without excuse because of the witness of Christians like you and me.

The faith of Noah was not based on religion, spiritism, or old wives' tales. Remember, since faith is a noun, it must be based on something or someone. Noah was not acting on a hunch or man's advice. He listened to the voice of God that "warned" him, and convicted him to act on "things not seen." For at the time there was no sign of a flood or any related event. His action was motivated by faith and faith alone, not by any reasoned calculation of the probabilities based on the best available evidence. In the Bible, Noah is the first man to be called righteous (Genesis 6:9). He was right with God because he took God at His word. He had faith to believe what God said, and he acted accordingly.

It takes faith for a man to build a boat on dry land, believing that it would save all that sought shelter from a danger that no one had ever heard of up till that time. It will take the same type of faith for us to evangelize the world today. We must warn them of an unimaginable danger.

Since Noah stood alone during the dispensation of government, we can only compare him to faithful men of other times, such as Enoch. In reality, we can only preach what has affected us inwardly.

Noah	**Enoch**
Preached righteousness	Preached judgment
Preached the way of salvation	Preached the judgment that his son bore witness to
By faith, Noah prepared the ark of safety	By faith, Enoch reaped the benefit of walking with God

To quote the senior pastor of my church, Ananias Holland, "Faith must be linked to knowledge to be exercised and grow." It is true that a man cannot believe what he does not know. That is a clear and self-evident axiom. Even if I have heard of a thing all my life and do not know it, I cannot believe it. Nevertheless, the problem in the church today is that our faith is like that of the fuller, who when asked what he believed, said "I believe what the church believes." What does the church believe? The church believes what I believe." And pray what does the church believe? Why, we both believe the same thing." The reality is that this man believed nothing, except that the church was right, but in what he did not know. It is futile that such a man may say, "I am a believer," yet our churches are full of members who are in that position. They are not able to respond in an appropriate fashion when challenged. No man's faith is a sure faith if he does not know what he believes. The apostle Paul has said in Romans 10:14-17,

> *How then shall they call on him in whom they have not believed? And how shall they believe in him of whom they have not heard? And how shall they hear without a preacher? And how shall they preach, except they be sent? As it is written, how beautiful are the feet of them that preach the gospel of peace, and bring glad tidings of good things! But they have not all obeyed the gospel. For Esaias saith, Lord who hath believed our report? So then faith cometh by hearing and hearing by the word of God.*

> *Study to shew thyself approved unto God, a workman that needeth not to be ashamed, rightly dividing the word of truth* (II Timothy 2:15).

It is necessary that a man must know the Word of God to have true faith. I must add that today he must know both the written and the Living Word, for faith has come. Today we are too quick to attach the word "faith" to any doctrine or creed. We need to heed the words of Jesus when He said in John 5:39-42,

> *Search the scriptures; for in them ye think ye have eternal life; and they are they which testify of me. And ye will not come to me, that ye might have life. I receive no honor from men. But I know you, that ye have not the love of God in you.*

If the Lord were to respond to this dilemma today, I believe many would be as convicted by the latter three verses of the statement above as were the people who physically heard Jesus' words.

Active faith consists of three things (1) knowledge, (2) affirmation, and (3) affiance, or the laying hold of the knowledge to which we give unanimity, and making it our own. We can see that quality in both Enoch and Noah, as the previous chart illustrates. Each man acted according to his faith, although their missions were distinctly different. The differences reflect that God required a different act from each man according to the particular dispensation.

The Faith That Pleases God

To this point I have shared my thoughts on what faith is. I have also stated that without faith it is impossible to please God. Now, I will ask a question: Have you got the faith that pleases God? To please God you must only know that "God is and He is a rewarder of them who diligently seek Him," but you must believe it. We must agree to the verity of God. You are not allowed to believe fragments of the Scriptures but must accept them willingly and wholeheartedly. True faith gives full assent to the verbal inerrancy of the Scriptures. It sees the Trinity, which it cannot understand, and believes it. All three of the patriarchs, mentioned to date in this book, gave full, free, and enthusiastic affirmation to the words spoken to them by God.

Faith also sees the atoning sacrifice that is difficult to understand and believes it because God said it. Whether the words from the Bible contain threats, promises, proverbs, precepts, or blessings, we embrace them as the truth. However, a man can have knowledge and assent, and yet not possess saving faith. In James 2:17 it says,

Even so faith, if it hath not works is dead, being alone.

The essential part that set Abel, Enoch, and Noah apart

was their commitment to the truth. You must take hold of it as being yours, and rest on it for your salvation. For example, it will not save you to *know* that Jesus Christ is a Savior, but it will save you if you *trust* Him to be your Savior. You will not be delivered from the wrath to come by believing that His atonement is sufficient, but you are saved if you trust in what He did for you. Jesus came, shed His blood on Calvary, died for all mankind, and was raised from the dead by the Holy Spirit. The quintessence, the "meat" of faith, lies in humbly submitting oneself to the promise. When saving a drowning man, the air in the life preserver is important, the act of throwing it to the potential victim is also important, but it is all irrelevant if the drowning man does not clutch on to it.

To this point we have seen where one man's act of faith and subsequent death put him in a position where his blood is permanently likened to Jesus. Another's faith allowed him to escape death altogether. And Noah's faith led to the continuance of the human race. The question is now—do you have faith? It's not sufficient to have the dead faith that James alluded to; we need the overcoming kind of faith that John refers to in I John 5:4-5. Ironically, in today's churches that profess to be "faith-based," people are actually defeated by the "test" of the genuineness of their faith, as seen in the epistle of James.

The half-brother of Jesus said that: "God tests our faith by the trials that we endure," James 1:1-12. He lists a twofold result; development of patience in this life, and the waiting for the "crowning" later. God does not test our faith with evil, but He will permit us to be tested by the enemy. However, the primary evil comes from within us; James 1:14 identifies our flesh as the "enticer." God tests our faith by His written and Living Word, and not by man's words. James 1:22-27 sets forth the relationship between knowledge, affirmation, and affiance. The fact is that *doing*, not doctrine, is the final test; knowing is not enough.

• God tests our faith by our attitude and action in respect to how we treat others, James 2:1-13.

• God tests our faith by our works, James 2:14-26. Abraham is used as an illustration; I will bring this out in the next chapter.

• God tests our faith by the theology of the tongue; specifically our own tongue, James 3. The tongue reveals the context of our heart.

• God tests our faith by asking whether we are lovers of the world's system. James 4,5. He points out the vacuity of worldliness; the vexation of the rich, and the vapidness of both in relation to the value of the imminent return of Jesus Christ.

Chapter 10

The Willingness of Faith

When the Son of man shall come in his glory, and all the holy angels with him, then shall he sit upon the throne of his glory; and before him shall be gathered all nations; and he shall separate them one from another, as a shepherd divideth his sheep from the goats; and he shall set the sheep on his right hand, but the goats on the left. Then shall the King say unto them on his right hand, come, ye blessed of my Father, inherit the kingdom prepared for you from the foundations of the world; for I was hungered, and ye gave me meat; I was thirsty, and ye gave me drink; I was a stranger and yet took me in; naked, and ye clothed me; I was sick and ye visited me; I was in prison and yet came unto me. Then shall the righteous answer him saying, Lord when saw we thee hungered and fed thee or thirsty and gave thee drink? When saw we thee a stranger and took thee in or naked and clothed thee? Or when saw we thee sick or in prison and came unto thee? And the King shall answer and say unto them, verily I say unto you, in as much as ye have done it unto the least of these my brethren, ye have done it unto me. Then shall he say also unto them on the left hand, depart from me, ye cursed, into everlasting fire, prepared for the devil and his angels. For I was hungered and ye gave me not meat; I was thirsty and ye gave me no drink; I was a stranger and ye took me not in; naked and ye clothed me not; sick and in prison and yet visited me not. Then shall they also answer him saying, verily I say unto you, in as much as ye did not to one of the least of these, ye did it not to me. And these shall go away into everlasting punishment; but the righteous into life eternal (Matthew 25:31-46).

The text above reveals that during the great tribulation, the 144,000 Jews, sealed at the time, will go out over the entire world to preach the Gospel of the kingdom. The living are encouraged to receive Christ as the sacrifice for their sins, and they are to be ready for His immediate coming. Some nations will reject Jesus, and their fate will be sealed. Those who accept the Lord will give evidence of their faith by their accepting of the message. The prize that awaits those who repent and turn to Christ is that they will be allowed to enter the millennium.

This is not a lesson about salvation as we know it today; for one thing, it is not concerning individuals but nations. Also, the term "brethren" is not about mankind in general, but those who preach the kingdom message. Finally, the spiritual lesson that is relevant to this manuscript is that those who receive the rewards are not seeking them (notice the befuddled query by the men in v. 44; they were unaware of the merit of their deed). At the end of the last chapter, I emphasized that our works are to reflect the faith that is in our "inner man." Nevertheless, it is important that we know that God is "a rewarder...," yet we must strive to accomplish His will without looking to receive tit for tat. Instead, we have the assurance of God's promises to reward us, even if we do not receive them in this life.

During the dispensation of promise, that is exactly what Abraham did;

By faith Abraham, when he was called to go out into a place which he should after receive for an inheritance, obeyed; and he went out, not knowing whither he went. By faith he sojourned in the land of promise, as in a strange country, dwelling in tabernacles with Isaac and Jacob, the heirs with him of the same promise; for he looked for a city which hath foundations, whose builder and maker is God. Through faith also Sarah herself received strength to conceive seed, and was delivered of a child when she was past age, because she judged him faithful who had promised. Therefore sprang there even of one, and him as good as dead, so many as the stars of the sky in multitude, and as the sand which is by the sea shore innumerable. These all died in faith, not having received the promises, but having seen them afar off, and were persuaded of them, and embraced them, and confessed that they were strangers and pilgrims on the earth. For they that say such things declare plainly that they seek a country. And truly, if they had been mindful of that country from whence they came out, they might have had opportunity to have re-turned. But now they desire a better country, that is, a heavenly; wherefore God is not ashamed to be called their God; for he hath prepared for them a city. By faith Abraham, when he was tried, offered up Isaac; and that he had received the promises offered up his only begotten son (Hebrews 11:8-17).

The above text states that father Abraham "looked for a city..." that history tells us he never received. Nevertheless, this dispensation illustrates the willingness of faith. What was this patriarch willing to do? He was willing to worship God. Through his life we can see that worship leads to obedience; it leads us to work for God. The result is that we do what God wants us to do. In line with this motivating force, rewards be-come secondary to our representing the glory of our Lord

Jesus Christ. We too must become kingdom-minded. If we seek to emulate Abram, who became Abraham, we will likewise obey God and erect an altar everywhere we go.

And the Lord appeared unto Abram and said, unto thy seed will I give this land; and there built he an altar unto the Lord, who appeared unto him. And he removed from thence unto a mountain on the east of Bethel, and pitched his tent, having Bethel on the west, and Hai on the east, and there he built an altar unto the Lord and called upon the name of the Lord (Genesis 12:7-8).

Everywhere this man went, he built an altar. Whether he went into the lands of Shechem or to the plains of Moreh, he erected altars honoring his God. He worshipped God by faith, and he was willing to obey God by faith. Did his obedience cost him? Yes, it cost him dearly, as it says in Hebrews 11:18-19

Of whom it was said, that in Isaac shall thy seed be called; accounting that God was able to raise him up, even from the dead; from whence also he received him in a figure.

The account of this aborted sacrifice of his son Isaac has been told innumerable times by his spiritual seed over the years. It has been used to emphasize the power of this man's faith. However, the effect on his family has not been told to the extent that it should be. I believe that the effect on his family was tragically irreversible. Considering that his wife, Sarah, died soon after this event, it is possible that she was devastated that either God would make such a request or her husband was losing his mind. Then, consider also that there is no biblical account of Isaac ever speaking to his father again. Despite the cost, Abraham was willing to obey the request of his God. Why? He worshipped God by faith!

Another thing we can learn from the patriarchs of this dispensation is that walking by faith will cause us all to recognize that as children of God we are just pilgrims and strangers down here on this earth. Nevertheless, faith gives us the ability to look to the future; witness the others listed during this age in Hebrews 11:20-22,

> *By faith Isaac blessed Jacob and Esau concerning things to come. By faith, Jacob when he was dying, blessed both the sons of Joseph; and worshipped, leaning upon the top of his staff. By faith Joseph, when he died, made mention of the departing of the children of Israel; and gave commandment concerning his bones.*

They all looked to the future promises of God, but each one had to endure an inglorious end to their lives.

Looking closer at v. 13, the author breaks off his treatment of Abraham for a moment to engage in some general remarks about "all these people." The reference to "all" allows for no exceptions, and it reflects a pattern in the lives of "all" that died exercising their faith, who did not possess what was promised. They all knew what they were promised, but they died without realizing the individual blessings. We must be careful in how we view this because the writer has already said that Abraham and Sarah (v. 11) did receive the child of their desires.

> *For when God made promise to Abraham, because he could swear by no greater, he swore by himself. Saying, surely blessing I will bless thee, and multiplying I will multiply thee. And so, after he had patently endured, he obtained the promise* (Hebrews 6:13-15).

Isaac was born from the union of a father who is described by the Word "as good as dead," and was nurtured in the "dead womb" of Sarah. However, the promise meant more than that. Actually, it was the fullness of the blessing that was in mind in Hebrews 11:13. The best thing that happens to all saints is

83

that, every now and then, we see a glimpse of heaven. Or we "see" what God has in store for us.

For example, anticipating the next chapter, we will see that though Moses prayed to enter the Promised Land, God would only let him "see" it.

> *But the Lord was wroth with me for your sakes, and would not hear me; and the Lord saith unto me, let it suffice thee; speak no more unto me of this matter. Get thee up unto the top of Pisgah, and lift up thine eyes westward, and northward, and southward, and eastward, and behold it with thine eyes; for thou shalt not go over this Jordan. But charge Joshua and encourage him and strengthen him; for he shall go over before this people, and he shall cause them to inherit the land which thou shalt see. So we abode in the valley over against Behpeor* (Deut. 3:26-29).

> *And Moses went up from the plains of Moab unto the mountains of Nebo, to the top of Pisgah that is over against Jericho. And the Lord showed him all the land of Gilead, unto Dan, and all Napthtali, and the land Ephraim, and Manasseh, and all the land of Judah, unto the utmost sea, and the south, and the plain of the valley of Jericho, the city of palm trees, unto Zoar. And the Lord said unto him, this is the land which I swore unto Abraham, unto Isaac, and unto Jacob, saying I will give it unto thy seed; I have caused thee to see it with thine eyes, but thou shalt not go over thither* (Deut. 34:1-4).

"See" can be used to denote various kinds of sight. Here it is used in the context of an operation of faith that is in the mind, and the word is slanted toward the inner awareness of what the promises meant. The latter term means those living in a country to which they do not belong. To "see" we must persevere in holiness, for this is a requirement of having the faith that pleases God. Today, many of us resemble the Titanic, because in fine, smooth weather we give an impregnable appearance, but when the storms of life come, we sink into the depths. In good company, in evangelical drawing rooms, in pious parlors, in chapels and vestries, we are pictures of victorious Christians, but when a little persecution comes, we are exposed for who we really are. However, true to our deceptive natures, when the storm is past, we are as pious as before. How many times have we heard of "great men of faith," who when confronted with a serious illness, secretly sought the aid of a physician. In reality, the only thing that they should be ashamed of is their hypocrisy. Imagine how they would respond if they faced being burnt at the stake for their belief. Some of these very shepherds would run away and leave their flocks to their own devices. This, my brothers and sisters is not faith at all.

> *But blessed are your eyes, for they see; and your ears, for they hear. For verily I say unto you that many prophets and righteous men have desire to see those things which ye see and have not seen them and to hear those things which ye hear and have not heard them* (Matthew 13:16-17).

Actually, your faith is greater than theirs for he that has faith must renounce his own righteousness and try their spirits as the Bible teaches in I John 4:1-3,

> *Beloved, believe not every spirit but try the spirits whether they are of God because many false prophets are gone out into the world. Hereby know ye the Spirit of God. Every spirit that confesseth that Jesus Christ is come in the flesh is of God, and every spirit that confesseth not that Jesus Christ is come in the flesh is not of God; and this is that spirit of antichrist; whereof ye have heard that it should come, and even now already is it in the world.*

Now the Spirit speaketh expressly that in the latter times some shall depart from the faith, giving heed to seducing spirits and doctrines of devils; speaking lies in hypocrisy; having their conscience seared with a hot iron (I Tim. 4:1).

If they trust in their works, their works are likened to that of an antichrist, and it is the Word that accuses them, not me. True faith may be known by this: it has great esteem for the person of Jesus Christ. Jesus must have your all or nothing at all. If you have the willingness of faith, you can say: "Nothing in my hand I bring. Simply to the cross I cling."

This is only half the story; for we do have something to look forward to because salvation is not only a past experience and a present reality, but also a future hope;

To an inheritance incorruptible, and undefiled, and that fadeth not away, reserved in heaven for you. Who are kept by the power of God through faith unto salvation ready to be revealed in the last time (I Peter 1:4-5).

The apostle of hope, Peter says it succinctly. He teaches that an inheritance by its very nature is something that will be received at some point in the future. In this case, the inheritance is incorruptible, undefiled, and unfading.

Abraham and the others in the hall of fame of faith knew by faith that the promises of this world cannot meet these conditions. For example, as with Esau's promised inheritance, an earthly inheritance can be traded or stolen or worse, removed from a predecessors will. (See Genesis 25:27-38).

Since our inheritance is reserved for us in heaven, it is not subject to the kind of uncertainties that human's face with their inheritance. Because our heavenly Father is faithful and always keeps His word, we can be certain that if we do not receive our promised desserts in this life, then we can be certain that they await us in glory.

Chapter 11

The Widening of Faith

In the fifth dispensation we can see "the faith" that had materialized into a religious movement under the influence of Abraham now, through the children of Israel, expanded its influence in the world. I will refer to this as the widening of faith. Specifically, in the persons of Moses, Joshua, and Rehab, Hebrews 11 tells how faith worked in the lives of these godly individuals.

First let us look at Moses who represents the sacrificing naturally expected of a saint.

By faith Moses, when he was born, was hid three months of his parents because they saw he was a proper child; and they were not afraid of the kings' commandment. By faith Moses, when he was come to years, refused to be called the son of Pharaoh's daughter. Choosing rather to suffer affliction with the people of God, than to enjoy the pleasures of sin for a season; esteeming the reproach of Christ greater riches than the treasures in Egypt; for he had respect unto the recompense of the reward. By faith he forsook Egypt, not fearing the wrath of the king; for he endured as seeing him who is invisible. Through faith he kept the Passover, and the sprinkling of blood, lest he that destroyed the firstborn should touch them. By faith they passed through the Red

Sea as by dry land; which the Egyptians assaying to do were drowned (Hebrews 11:23-29).

The name Moses means "drawn forth," or "taken out of the water a son," it describes his birth to godly parents who were willing to take a real stand for God. Faith was involved in the very birth of Moses (Exodus 2:10-21; Acts 7:20-38; Hebrews 11:24-25). It would take a volume of words to expound the virtues and vicissitudes of Moses' roles as historian, orator, leader, statesmen, legislator, and patriot. However, his greatest honor was the privilege of being "pleasing to God." Whereas, Abraham was called a "Friend of God" (James 2:23), someone besides Abraham saw Christ's day and rejoiced—Moses did. Moses had faith to act in obedience to God. Contrast that with those today who cry "I believe, I believe," but they do nothing. His actions are chronicled in the verses above, but his life can be viewed under very extraordinary circumstances.

Moses lived for 120 years, a period that can be divided into three sections of forty years each:
• The first forty years Moses learned to be somebody.
• The next forty years he learned to be nobody.
• The last forty years he learned that God was the God of everybody.

Moses' personal exodus led him to experience:
• The moment that he fully turned to God.
• The moment that he broke with the world.
• The moment that he took a covenant with God.

From his life we can learn that it is not enough to refuse to follow the world, but we must choose to follow God by repenting. We must back up our negative lives with positive affirmations of God.

From this example we can see the oneness that a person of

faith can have with Christ. Notice the similarities between Moses and Jesus:

- Both were saved from the perils of infancy (Ex. 2:2-10 and Matt. 2:14, 15).
- Both were tempted but overcame evil (Ex. 7:11 and Matt. 4:1).
- Both fasted for forty days (Ex. 34:28 and Matt. 4:2).
- Both had power to control the sea (Ex. 14:21 and Matt. 8:26).
- Both fed a multitude (Ex. 16:26 and Matt. 14:20, 21)
- Both had their faces radiated (Ex. 34:35 and Matt. 17:2).
- Both endured murmuring (Ex. 15:24 and Mark 7:2).
- Both were mighty intercessors (Ex. 32:32 and John 17).
- Both spoke as oracles of God (Deut. 18:18 and John 7:46).
- Both had 70 helpers (Num. 11:16, 17 and Luke 10:1).
- Both established memorials (Ex. 12:14 and Luke 22:19).
- Both reappeared after death (Matt. 17:3 and Acts 1:30.

Consider this, whose faith do we see during the Exodus? Do we see the faith of the people? No! We see the faith of one man, Moses. He went down to the water's edge and smote it with the rod. He acted in faith, and the waters opened up so that the Hebrew children could walk across on dry land. Then they sang the song of Moses. The people identified with Moses, but this is the story of his faith. That is why the Bible characterizes this by saying,

He made known his ways unto Moses, his acts unto the children of Israel (Psalms 103:7).

At the age of 120, while "his eyes were not dimmed," God

called His faithful servant to climb the lonely mountain of Nebo, where, Moses was kissed to sleep and buried by God— the only man to have God as his undertaker (Deut. 34:6). However, his contribution to the widening influence of faith consisted in his writing the first five books of the Bible, which set forth the full flowering of the law of God in the content of the foundational series of events that began with the Exodus and climaxed at Mt. Sinai. It was Moses who led a people that were liberated and redeemed by God's grace. The moral vitality of the environment created by men obeying the Law turned even the scenery against evil and gave men something tangible to believe in. His writings also gave us grand descriptions of the origin and fall of man, as told in the book of Genesis. Moses may have been unsuccessful, as men see it, but he will receive his just reward in heaven.

Joshua's Faith

By faith the walls of Jericho fell down, after they were compassed about seven days (Hebrews 11:30).

Though Joshua is not mentioned by name in the above verse, he is the main character. In Joshua we see the watch of faith. General Joshua had that kind of faith. The facts of the miraculous destruction of the walls of Jericho is narrated in the book named after him.

Joshua 6 tells the story of the fall of Jericho, but Joshua's faith was emboldened by an appearance by the reincarnate Christ:

And it came to pass, when Joshua was by Jericho, that he lifted up his eye and looked, and behold, there stood a man over against him with his sword drawn in his hand; and Joshua went unto him, and said unto him, art thou for us or for our adversaries? And he said, nay; but as captain of the host of the Lord am I now come. And Joshua fell on his face to the earth and did worship and said unto him, what saith my lord unto his servant? And the captain of the Lord's host said unto Joshua. Loose thy shoe from off they foot; for the place whereon thou standeth is holy. And Joshua did so (Joshua 5:13-15).

While the destruction of the walls was produced by the power of God, it may be asked "how is it by faith?" The faith referred to is plainly that of Joshua, believing God had spoken to him:

And ye shall compass the city all ye men of war, and go round about the city once. Thus shalt thou do six days. And seven priests shall bear before the ark seven trumpets of ram's horns; and the seventh day ye shall compass the city seven times, and the priests shall blow with the trumpets. And it shall come to pass that when they make a long blast with the ram's horn, and when ye hear the sound of the trumpet, all the people shall shout with a great shout; and the wall of the city shall fall down flat, and the people shall ascend up every man straight before him (Joshua 6:3-5).

Persevering faith enabled Joshua and the children of Israel to do what otherwise they could not have done. To their credit, the people also believed the words that were reported to them by their captain.

The writer of the book of Hebrews included this story to aid the Hebrew Christians who were engaged in a cause that appeared to be as hopeless as the capture of this great city. The daunting task they faced was to overcome Judaism, paganism, false religion, and worldly powers. The preaching of the Gospel, today, along with the prayers of the saints, and our patience under manifold and severe afflictions, in the estimation of human reasoning, makes our defeat seem inevitable.

However, faith renders the impossible attainable. What faith? Our faith makes us well-fitted to obtain the goal of winning souls. Every individual Christian in "working out his own salvation," must contend with spiritual enemies in order for him/her to do his/her part in the propagation of Christianity throughout the world. We need to:

> *And beside this, giving all diligence, add to you faith virtue and to virtue knowledge; and to knowledge temperance; and to temperance patience; and to patience godliness; and to godliness, brotherly kindness; and to brotherly kindness, charity. For if these things be in you, and abound, they make you that ye shall neither be barren nor unfruitful in the knowledge of our Lord Jesus Christ* (II Peter 1:5-8).

In doing so, we are guaranteed to be abundantly fruitful, in spite of the barriers that face us, which are more difficult than the physical walls Joshua faced. Faith can do it; nothing but faith can do it.

> *By faith the harlot Rehab perished not with them that believed not, when she had received the spies with peace* (Hebrews 11:31).

Now we come to something that has confounded men since the plan of salvation was instituted—how mere faith in God can override our evil acts so that God can redeem us. Rehab's faith spared her the fate of the other citizens of Jericho. From her life we can see that God doesn't view any group of people as being outside the range of His grace. The reason is that God sees us all as sinners, and when anyone turns to Him, God will save them.

Rahab's testimony is recorded in Joshua 2:9-11,

> *And she said unto the men, I know that the Lord hath*

*given you the land, and that your terror is fallen upon us
and that all the inhabitants of the land faint because of
you. For we have heard how the Lord dried up the water of
the Red Sea for you when ye came out of Egypt; and what
ye did unto the two kings of the Amorites, that were on the
other side of Jordan, Sihon, and Og, whom ye utterly destroyed. And as soon as we had heard these things, our
hearts did melt, neither did there remain any more
courage in any man because of you; for the Lord your
God, he is God in heaven above, and in earth beneath.*

This (see Hebrews 11:11b) is a strange statement considering that she was both a foreigner and a prostitute, but it reveals the fact that God did not arbitrarily destroy the city. The
fact is, for 40 years word had filtered into Jericho about the exploits of the Israelites. Others may have believed the facts, but
they didn't believe in God. Rahab did, however, and she lived,
and because the others did not believe, they perished. The
whole city, save one, missed their opportunity to experience
the grace and mercy of God. This principle still applies today.

*The Lord is not slack concerning his promise, as some men
count slackness, but is longsuffering to us-ward, not
willing that any should perish but that all should come to
repentance* (II Peter 3:9).

This wonder of faith mystifies Satan as well. Jude speaks of the
error of Balaam, as opposed to the way of Balaam (II Peter
2:15), or the doctrine of Balaam (Rev. 2:14). Listen to Jude:

*Woe unto them for they have gone in the way of Cain, and
ran greedily after the error of Balaam for reward and
perished in the gainsaying of Core* (Jude 11)

The error that Jude addresses is that Balaam thought that
God would have to punish Israel for their sins. However, he

did not recognize that there is a morality that is above natural morality. He thought a righteous God had to curse Israel (Numbers 23-24). He was wrong, He, like Satan, was unaware of the morality of the Cross;

> *And as Moses lifted up the serpent in the wilderness, even so must the Son of man be lifted up; that whosoever believeth in him should not perish, but have eternal life. For God so loved the world, that he gave his only begotten Son that whosoever believeth in him should not perish but have everlasting life. For God sent not his Son into the world to condemn the world; but the world through him might be saved. He that believeth on him is not condemned; but he that believeth not is condemned already, because he hath not believed in the name of the only begotten Son of God* (John 3:14-18).

What was symbolized in the Old Testament became a reality in the New Testament because faith came. God is still both Just and the Justifier of the believing sinner.

The apostates today make the same mistake. Some err because they cannot believe that the sacrifice of Jesus is not enough to save everyone. They think a man must do something worthy of salvation, despite Ephesians 2:8-10. Some go to the other extreme and deny their own sinful status, but if you notice that in Hebrews, Rahab is still referred to as a harlot. The thief on the Cross that was saved, died before he could change his status. Consider also that no less than the apostle Paul referred to himself as the "chief of sinners." The reality is that where most charismatic churches have no problem with the theological phrase progressive sanctification; they object vehemently if you use the phrase progressive holiness. Ironically, both terms are translated from the same Greek word, *hagiasmos*. Or, to put it another way, they are two heads to the same coin. I agree with Paul:

God forbid, yea, let God be true, but every man a liar; as it is written, that thou mightest be justified in thy sayings and mightest overcome when thou art judged (Romans 3:4).

Clearly God ended this dispensation by showing the ability of men to be saved was extended beyond the seed of Abraham, and is not available to the whole world. Praise His Holy Name! We are all eligible to receive the "gift of God." We will see in the next age that; while "the gift" is free, there is a cost to be paid.

Chapter 12

The War of Faith, Part 1

And what shall I more say? For the time would fail me to tell of Gideon and of Barak and of Samson, and of Jephthae; of David also, and Samuel, and of the prophets; who through faith subdued kingdoms, wrought righteousness, obtained promises, stopped the mouths of lions. Quenched the violence of fire, escaped the edge of the sword, out of weakness were made strong, waxed valiant in fight, turned to flight the armies of the aliens. Women received their dead raised to life again; and others were tortured, not accepting deliverance, that they might obtain a better resurrection. And others had trial of cruel mockings and scourgings, yea, moreover of bonds and imprisonment. They were stoned, they were sawn asunder, were tempted, were slain with the sword; they wandered about in sheepskins and goatskins; being destitute, afflicted, tormented; (of whom the world was not worthy) they wandered in deserts, and in mountains, and in dens and caves of the earth. And these all, having obtained a good report through faith, received not the promise. God having provided some better thing for us, that they without us should not be made perfect (Hebrews 11:32-40).

As the influence of the people of God expanded, so too did the resistance they encountered. The second part of this dispensation reflects the war of faith. In verse 32, we see different leaders of Israel, some kings and some judges, but they were all leaders engaged in a war for God. Each of them won their personal battle of faith. Because the author of this book of Hebrews does not detail their exploits, neither will I at this time. It is not so relevant what they did, but how they did it—by faith.

There is also a reference to Daniel's story in verse 33, although he is not mentioned by name. The remaining verses of this chapter list the faith of "others." They are those who were martyred for their beliefs. Upon the lives of these martyrs was the bridge built that led from the fifth to the sixth dispensation, or from Law to Grace.

These men and women did not win their victories on the battlefields. They did not "do their thing" before great audiences of cheering fans but often before the jeers and mocking of their enemies. These are the "others" and if you want or need heroes, they are worthy of your admiration. We don't even know their names for sure, but they all suffered cruel and inhuman deaths. Notice the contrasts; in verse 33 it was said that these believers "subdued kingdoms, wrought righteousness, obtained promises, etc. and escaped the edge of the sword, but the later saints were subdued and slain with the sword. These heroes of the faith went through these afflictions "by faith." While many have demonstrated their faith by winning battles, why have multitudes suffered for their faith?

Peter deals with this question by saying:

Wherein ye greatly rejoice, though now for a season, if need be, ye are in heaviness through manifold temptations; that the trial of your faith, being much more precious than of gold that perisheth, though it be tried with fire, might be found unto praise and honor and glory at the appearing of Jesus Christ; whom having not seen, ye love; in whom though now ye see him not, yet believing ye rejoice with joy unspeakable and full of glory; receiving the end of your faith, even the salvation of your souls (I Peter 1:6-9).

Paul addresses this dilemma by saying:

Who now rejoice in my sufferings for you and fill up that which is behind of the afflictions of Christ in my flesh for his body's sake, which is the church. Whereof I am made a minister, according to the dispensation of God which is given to me for you to fulfill the word of God; even the mystery which hath been hid from ages and from generations, but now is made manifest to his saints; to whom God would make known what is the riches of the glory of this mystery among the Gentiles; which is Christ in you, the hope of glory. Whom we preach, warning every man and teaching every man in all wisdom; that we may present every man perfect in Christ Jesus; whereunto I also labor, striving according to his working, which worketh in me mightily (Col. 1:24-29).

Notice that it says that they "received not the promise." If the promise to them was prosperity, then God failed to deliver and His ability to do so should be questioned. This cannot be, for we know that not only is God all powerful, but He is veracious:

That by two immutable things in which it was impossible for God to lie, we might have a strong consolation, who have fled for refuge to lay hold upon the hope set before us (Hebrews 6:18).

Therefore, the promise spoken of must be God's promise

that He will raise them up and that there will be a kingdom established here on earth. Why? The answer is in Hebrews 11:40. God has us in mind. The church had to be established and completed.

Faith leads to obedience and the price required is often painful.

Then said Jesus unto his disciples, if any man will come after me, let him deny himself and take up his cross and follow me (Matthew 16:24).

Can your faith compare to the apostle Paul's? Let us look at the things that he felt set his ministry on such a high standard:

I say again, let no man think me a fool; if otherwise yet as a fool receive me, that I may boast myself a little. That which I speak, I speak it not after the Lord, but as it were foolishly, in this confidence of boasting. Seeing that many glory after the flesh, I will glory also. For ye suffer fools gladly, seeing yourselves are wise. For ye suffer, if a man bring you into bondage, if a man devour you, if a man take of you, if a man exalt himself, if a man smite you on the face. I speak as concerning reproach, as though we had been weak. Howbeit whereinsoever any is bold (I speak foolishly,) I am bold also. Are they Hebrews? So am I. Are they Israelites? So am I. Are they the seed of Abraham? So am I. Are they ministers of Christ? (I speak as a fool) I am more; in labors more abundant, in stripes above measure, in prisons more frequent, in deaths oft. Of the Jews five times I received forty stripes save one. Thrice was I beaten with rods, once was I stoned, thrice I suffered shipwreck, a night and a day I have been in the deep; in journeyings often in perils of waters, in perils of robbers, in perils by mine own countrymen, in perils by the heathen, in perils in the city, in perils in the wilderness, in perils in the sea, in perils among false brethren; in weariness and painfulness, in watchings often, in hunger and thirst, in fastings often, in cold and nakedness. Beside those things that are without, that which cometh upon me daily, the care of all the churches. Who is weak, and I am not weak? Who is offended, and I burn not? If I must need glory, I will glory of the things which concern mine infirmities. The God and Father of our Lord Jesus Christ, which is blessed for evermore, knoweth that I lie not. In Damascus the governor under Aretas the king kept the city of the Damascenes with a garrison, desirous to apprehend me; and through a window in a basket was I let down by the wall, and escaped his hands (II Corinthians 11:16-33).

The unwillingness to suffer for His beliefs was a principle that did not exist in the mind of our Lord. Just being in the Father's will made the bitterest cup sweeter and made his heavy load lighter. So far from obedience being difficult to Him, merely as obedience, it was His "meat," "drink," and "purpose." He was single-minded when it came to doing the will of His Father, and He was committed to finish His work. He also invites us to:

Come unto me all ye that labor and are heavy laden, and I will give you rest. Take my yoke upon you and learn of me; for I am meek and lowly in heart and ye shall find rest for your souls. For my yoke is easy, and my burden is light (Matthew 11:28-30).

Let me now set forth a painful reality and yet a biblical principle. We demonstrate that we have learned obedience when we are suffering, not when we are prospering. The difference is that when we are prospering, our learning is passive. God's desire for us is to learn by use and practice. The Greek word is *manthano*, which means to learn by observation or, as in the following verses, by actively living it out:

Not that I speak in respect of want; for I have learned, in whatsoever state I am, therewith to be content (Phil. 4:11).

But if any widow have children or nephews, let them first to shew piety at home and to requite their parents; for that is good and acceptable before God. And withal they learn to be idle, wandering about from house to house; and not only idle, but tattlers also and busybodies, speaking things which they ought not (I Timothy 5:4).

And let ours also learn to maintain good works for necessary uses, that they be not unfruitful (Titus 3:14).

This principle is so embedded in Scripture that even our Lord Jesus had to "learn."

Who in the days of his flesh, when he had offered up prayers and supplications with strong crying and tears unto him that was able to save him from death, and was heard in that he feared; though he were a Son, yet learned he obedience by the things he suffered; and being made perfect, he became the author of eternal salvation unto all them that obey him (Hebrews 5:7-9).

When it is said of us that we need to "learn obedience" by the things that we suffer, it can then be concluded that we have overcome our rebellious tendencies, and we have been disciplined into this state. However, that would be blasphemous to say the same of our Lord Jesus. His obedience was willing for who could have compelled Him. Nevertheless, had it been other than voluntary, it could not have served its purpose. If Jesus had obeyed reluctantly, it would not have served its purpose—to magnify and make honorable the divine law.

The language of our Lord's conduct was:

Then said I lo, I come; in the volume of the book it is written of me. I delight to do thy will, O my God; yea thy law is within my heart (Psalm 40:7-8).

By doing so, Jesus qualified as our High Priest. The law of the Levitical high priest was that we would offer gifts and sacrifices for the sins of Israel; the law of our great High Priest was that He would offer Himself as a sacrifice and a offering for us.

For every high priest taken from among men is ordained for men in things pertaining to God, that he may offer both gifts and sacrifices for sins; who can have compassion on the ignorant, and on them that are out of the way; for that he himself also is compassed with infirmity. And by reason hereof he ought as for the people, so also for himself, to offer for sins. And no man taketh this honor unto himself, but he that is called of God, as was Aaron. So also Christ glorified not himself to be made a high priest; but he that said unto him, Thou art my Son, today I have begotten thee. As he saith also in another place, Thou art a priest for ever after the order of Melchisedec (Hebrews 5:1-6).

Thus, Jesus became actively acquainted with obedience to this law by His suffering. This is one of the many passages which plainly show that the Son of God and Messiah are not synonyms. The Son of God is an essential and not an official appellation, which we will see more clearly in the following chapter.

Chapter 13

The Call of Faith

And it came to pass that as they went in the way a certain man said unto him Lord I will follow thee whithersoever thou goest. And Jesus said unto him, foxes have holes and birds of the air have nests; but the Son of man hath not where to lay his head. And he said unto another, follow me. But he said, Lord suffer me first to go and bury my father. Jesus said unto him, let the dead bury their dead; but go thou and preach the kingdom of God. And another also said, Lord I will follow thee but let me first go bid them farewell, which are at home at my house. And Jesus dais unto him, no man having put his hand to the plough, and looking back is fit for the kingdom of God (Luke 9:57-62).

And when he had called the people unto him with his disciples also, he said unto them, whosoever will come after me, let him deny himself and take up his cross and follow me. For whosoever will save his life shall lose it; but whosoever shall lose his life for my sake and the gospel's, the same shall have it. For what shall it profit a man if he shall gain the whole world and lose hi own soul? Or what shall a man give in exchange for his soul? Whosoever therefore shall be ashamed of me and of my words in this adulterous

103

and sinful generation; of him also shall the Son of man be ashamed, when he cometh in the glory of his Father with the holy angels (Mark 8:34-37).

Jesus gives three directions to those that seek to be His disciples:
1. Come to Me
2. Abide in Me
3. Follow Me.

However, He also tells them what price they must pay if they respond to his invitation. The requirements are
1. self-denial
2. sacrifice
3. suffering,
4. obedience

These are the minimum requisites for such an honorable profession. And I might add they are still mandated today.

I beseech you therefore, brethren, by the mercies of God that ye present your bodies a living sacrifice, holy, acceptable unto God, which is your reasonable service. And be not conformed to this world but be ye transformed by the renewing of your mind, that ye may prove what is that good and acceptable and perfect will of God (Romans 12:1).

The examples given in Luke's Gospel reflect Jesus' response to the alibis that men use to turn down the Lord's call—our self-interests overshadow the inward desire to do the will of God. What we can learn from their excuses is that we cannot follow Jesus if we are looking back favorably to the allures of this world. We must be willing to live by faith, walk by faith, and if necessary risk our lives because of faith, if it will further the cause of our Lord. We see this motivating factor in the life of apostle Paul,

I am crucified with Christ; nevertheless I live; yet not I but Christ liveth in me; and the life which I now live in the flesh I live by the faith of the Son of God, who loved me and gave himself for me (Galatians 2:20).

For this corruptible must put on incorruption and this mortal must put on immorality. So when this corruptible shall have put on incorruption and this mortal shall have put on immorality, then shall be brought to pass the saying that is written; death is swallowed up in victory. O death where is thy sting? O grave, where is the victory? The sting of death is sin; and the strength of sin is the law. But thanks be to God, which giveth us the victory through our Lord Jesus Christ. Therefore my beloved brethren be ye steadfast, unmovable, always abounding in the work of the Lord, forasmuch as ye know that your labor is not in vain in the Lord (I Cor. 15:53).

I protest by your rejoicing which I have in Christ Jesus our Lord, I will die daily (I Cor. 15:31).

But what things were gain to me, those I counted loss for Christ. Yea doubtless and I count all things but loss for the Excellency of the knowledge of Christ Jesus my Lord; for whom I have suffered the loss of all things, and do count them but dun, that I may win Christ. And be found in him, not mine own righteousness which is of the law, but that which is through the faith of Christ, the righteousness which is of God by faith; that I may know him and the power of his resurrection and the fellowship of his sufferings being made conformable unto his death; if by any means I might attain unto the resurrection of the dead (Phil 3:7).

The former Pharisee also says in Philippians 2:5, "Let this mind be in you, which was also in Christ Jesus."

Let us explore the mind of our Lord and Savior, Jesus Christ. We have seen an account of the Savior's mind-set in the last chapter, as revealed in Hebrews 5:7-9. It reveals that he "yet learned he obedience by the things which he suffered." It seems to tell us that the learning of obedience and the offering of the "prayers and supplications" for us were contemporaneous. The words "prayers" properly signifies Jesus' personal war against the opposing evil, while the word "supplications" denotes His plea for assistance under extreme distress. Therefore, we see our Lord indicating the intensity of His suffering and the passion of His devotional sentiments.

The prayers and the supplications were addressed to His heavenly Father when He prayed to "him that was able to save him from death." He knew that death, under the curse, would be the ultimate cost of His obedience, which He was actively learning during those trying times. Why did He have to go through this prolonged ordeal? Because it was necessary to fulfill what was written beforehand,

> *Think not that I am come to destroy the law or the prophets; I am come to destroy, but to fulfill* (Matt. 5:17).

To fulfill His mission, He had to be what He was called to be.

> *And being found in fashion as a man, he humbled himself, and became obedient unto death even the death of the cross* (Phil 2:8).

Of course, God could have prevented His only begotten Son from dying, but He could not do so and remain consistent with the economy of human salvation. Only after Jesus' paid the price for our salvation could God step in and bring Jesus back from the dead because the requirement for our salvation was the shed blood of the innocent Lamb. This was the final step that confirmed Jesus as the Messiah, for He had already been proclaimed the same by His baptism by John.

This is he that came by water and blood, even Jesus Christ not by water only but by water and blood. And it is the Spirit that beareth witness because the Spirit is truth. For there are three that bear record in Heaven, the Father, the Word, and the Holy Ghost; and these three are one. And there are three that bear witness in earth, the spirit and the water and the blood; and these three agree in one. If we receive the witness of men the witness of God is greater; for this is the witness of God which he hath testified of his Son (I John 5:6-9).

"Who in the days of his flesh" denotes more than the hours of agony that He spent in the Garden of Gethsemane and the six hours spent on the cross. They included all the days of His humiliation.

Who being in the form of God thought it not robbery to be equal with God; but made himself of no reputation and took upon him the form of a servant and was made in the likeness of men; and being found in fashion as a man he humbled himself and became obedient unto death even the death of the cross. Wherefore God also hath highly exalted him and given him a name which is above every name (Phil 2:6).

Among the other distinctive of "that Name" was the title given to Him—the Son of God. Isaiah 9:6 says,

For unto us a child is born, unto us a son is given and the government shall be upon his shoulder and his name shall be called Wonderful, Counselor, the mighty God, the everlasting Father, the Prince of Peace. "

Let me add to that verse three New Testaments verses.

For unto which of the angels said he at any time, Thou art my Son this day have I begotten thee? And again, I

will be to him a Father, and he shall be to me a Son? (Hebrews 1:5).

So also Christ glorified not himself to be made a high priest, but he that said unto him, thou art my Son today I have begotten thee (Hebrews 5:5).

But we see Jesus who was made a little lower than the angels for the suffering of death, crowned with glory and honor that he by the grace of God should taste death for every man. For it became him for whom are all things and by whom are all things in bringing many sons unto glory to make the captain of their salvation perfect through sufferings (Heb. 2:9).

All suffering is, to the human constitution, the object of repugnance and fear, and the human part of Jesus would react as most men would. However, our Lord was not afraid of being set aside by His Father, nor did he fear that his prayers would go unanswered, for He said,

And I knew that thou hearest me always; but because of the people which stand by I said it that they may believe that thou hast sent me (John 11:42).

In answer to His prayers, the Father not only supported His Son in His hour of crisis, but He ultimately completely delivered the innocent Jesus and returned Him to His glorified state.

Wherefore God also hath highly exalted him and given him a name which is above every name; that at the name of Jesus every knee should bow, of things in heaven and things in earth and things under the earth; and that every tongue should confess that Jesus Christ is Lord, to the glory of God the Father (Phil 2:9-11).

Thus, the first part of the Hebrews statement explains how the High Priest successfully, fulfilled the functions of His office. As a result, the intensity of His sufferings and the holiness of His character were manifested in His earnest supplications. Now He can challenge us with the words,

> *It is a faithful saying; for if we be dead with him we shall also live with him. If we suffer, we shall also reign with him, if we deny him, he also will deny us. If we believe not, yet he abideth faithful; he cannot deny himself* (II Timothy 2:11).

Remember that upon these words our eternal security rests, even if we are found unfaithful. Praise His Holy Name!

Having been made "perfect" through His unwavering obedience, He obtained all the merit, power, and authority necessary to execute the functions as our High Priest and by virtue of His accomplishments. That is what the writer meant when he said "and being made perfect...." He could then say, "he became the author of eternal salvation unto all them that obey him." Listen to the words of John Brown in his commentary on Hebrews,

> ...magnified and made honorable the divine law as to make it safe and wise, and just in the extreme Moral Governor, to pardon sin and save the sinner, from regard to this "obedience afforded of its excellence.... His investiture with that character, was not as a mere man, but the Son of God...His investiture was signalized by the peculiar solemnity of a divine oath."

In other words, it is consistent with Psalm 110:

> *The Lord said unto the Lord, sit thou at my right hand, until I make thine enemies thy footstool. The Lord shall send the rod of thy strength out of Zion; rule thou in the*

midst of thine enemies. Thy people shall be willing in the day of thy power, in the beauties of holiness from the womb of the morning; thou hast the dew of thy youth. The Lord hath sworn and will not repent. Thou art a priest for ever after the order of Melchizedek. The Lord at thy right hand shall strike through kings in the day of his wrath. He shall judge among the heathen, he shall fill the places with the dead bodies; he shall wound the heads over many countries. He shall drink of the brook in the way; therefore shall he lift up the head (Psalms 110:1-7).

Faith had come so that all of the Scriptures above, as well as others, could be fulfilled. After having digressed for a chapter, let us move forward in the exposition of the dispensational aspects of faith as revealed in Hebrews 11. Any teaching on faith as the tool to get wealth has not prepared the Church to move into the sixth dispensation that I have labeled the war of faith. Jude warned us,

Beloved when I gave all diligence to write unto you of the common salvation, it was needful for me to write unto you and exhort you that ye should earnestly contend for the faith which was once delivered unto the saints (Jude 3).

And Jesus questioned,

I tell you that he will avenge them speedily. Nevertheless when the Son of man cometh, shall he find faith on the earth? (Luke 18:8)

Chapter 14

The Suffering of Faith

There are times when God permits tribulation in our lives for the express purpose of helping us to grow into maturity. And I spent the last chapter detailing how our faith plays an important role making our pain more tolerable. We are to be thankful, in spite of the circumstances. Let the apostles testify, in their own words;

Who are kept by the power of God through faith unto salvation ready to be revealed in the last time. Wherein ye greatly rejoice, though now for a season, if need be ye are in heaviness through manifold temptations; that the trial of your faith being much more precious than of gold that perisheth, though it tried with fire might be found unto praise and honor and glory at the appearing of Jesus Christ (I Peter 1:5-7).

And not only so, but we glory in tribulations also knowing that tribulation worketh patience; and patience, experience, and experience hope. And hope maketh not ashamed because the love of God is shed abroad in our hearts by the Holy Ghost which is given unto us (Romans 5:3-5).

And we know that all things work together for good to them that love God, to them who are the called according

111

Faith Came—Now What?

to his purpose. For whom he did foreknow he also did pre-destinate to be conformed to the image of his Son, that he might be the firstborn among many brethren. Moreover whom he did predestinate, them he also called and whom he called them he also justified and whom he justified them he also glorified. What shall we then say to these things? If God be for us, who can be against us? He hat spared not his own Son but delivered him for us all, how shall he not with him also freely give us all things? Who shall lay any thing to the charge of God's elect? It is God that justifieth. Who is he that condemneth? It is Christ that died, yea rather that is risen again who is even at the right hand of God, who also maketh intercession for us. Who shall separate us from the love of Christ? Shall tribu-lation, or distress, or persecution, or famine, or nakedness, or peril, or sword? As it is written, for thy sake we are killed all the day long; we are accounted as sheep for the slaughter. Nay, in all these things we are more than con-querors through him that loved us. For I am persuaded that neither death nor life, nor angels, nor principalities, nor powers, nor things present, nor things to come (Romans 8:28-38).

Now thanks be unto God which always causeth us to tri-umph in Christ and maketh manifest the savor of his knowledge by us in every place, for we are unto God a sweet savor of Christ, in them that are saved and in them that perish. To the one we are the savor of death unto death and to the other the savor of life unto life. And who is sufficient for these things? For we are not as many, which corrupt the word of God; but as sincerity, but as of God in the sight of God speak we in Christ (II Cor. 2:14).

The later half of Hebrews 11 is an illustration of the many men and women who died for their faith. It was "by faith" that these many accounts were brought about. A revelation, made to the minds of the participants, led them to speak a word or do the action that put them in harm's way. While the first part of that chapter gave the examples of the power of faith enabling men to accomplish great feats, the later half is an illustration of the power of faith to enable saints to endure the severest trials and yet continue steadfast I their duty to God. While the modern day apostates point to the former examples, I believe equal time must be given to the later examples; that is if we are going to participate in the war of faith.

Let us look at the "others" that are referred to in the Hall of Faith. They are a set of believers who endured a horrendous array of tortures.

And others had trial of cruel mockings and scourgings, yea moreover of bonds and imprisonment. They were stoned, they were sawn asunder, were tempted, were slain with the sword; they wandered about in sheepskins and goatskins; being destitute, afflicted, tormented (Hebrews 11:36-37).

The reasons for their steadfastness amid these tortures is given in the previous verse,

Women received their dead raised to life again; and others were tortured, not accepting deliverance; that they might obtain a better resurrection (Hebrews 11:35).

These tortured souls refused deliverance that they might obtain a better resurrection than that which brought the dead back to life in this world. They sought a resurrection to life eternal! It deserves notice that this hope of a "better resurrection" is said of those who were tortured to death because they would not accept a present deliverance. In other words they volunteered to die rather than deny. They looked for hope from God to be raised up again by Him. Another said, in the face of death, "My brethren are dead under God's covenant of everlasting life." In the words of John Brown,

> It is a striking fact that these words are just as descriptive of what the Christian Church has undergone since the apostle wrote (referring to the tortures in Heb. 11:35-38) as they were of what the Jewish Church had undergone before he wrote.

The parenthetical expression at the beginning of the 38th verse really connects that time to now; "Of whom the world was not worthy." Ironically, their prosecutors thought them not worthy of the world, but the truth was, the world was not worthy of them.

> *Dearly beloved, I beseech you as strangers and pilgrims, abstain from fleshly lusts which war against the soul; having your conversation honest among the Gentiles, that whereas they speak against as evildoers, they may by your good works which they shall behold, glorify God in the day of visitation* (I Peter 2:11-12).

Truthfully speaking, the world could not bear a comparison to the Christ-centered minds of the children of God. We are charged to have a character far elevated above the rest of the world. The application to the saints is clear; we have much to do and we have much to suffer as Christians. Faith can enable us to suffer whatever is necessary. Harder still, not only are we to overcome the world, but we are to do so without complaining, according to the Scriptures.

> *As it is written, for thy sake we are killed all the day long; we are accounted as sheep for the slaughter. Nay, in all these things we are more than conquerors through him that loved us* (Romans 8:36-37).

The Suffering of Faith

*These things I have spoken unto you that in me ye might
have peace. In the world ye shall have tribulation; but be
of good cheer. I have overcome the world* (John 16:33).

*Rejoice evermore. Pray without ceasing. In everything
give thanks; for this is the will of God in Christi Jesus concerning you* (I Thess. 5:16-18).

Is the Lord insensitive to our needs? No! He has also said,

*The thief cometh not, but for to steal and to kill and to de-
stroy; I am come that they might have life and that they
might have it more abundantly. I am the good shepherd;
the good shepherd giveth his life for the sheep. But he that
is a hireling and not the shepherd, whose own sheep are
not, seeth the wolf coming an leaveth the sheep and fleeth;
and the wolf catcheth them and scattereth the sheep. The
hireling fleeth, because he is a hireling an careth not for
the sheep. I am the good shepherd, and know my sheep and
am known of mine* (John 10:10-14).

He has expressed His desire to bless us abundantly.
However, to give us the proper balance, Jesus warns us about
the world in John 10:10. In the latter verses, He warns against
the coming apostates, who He describes as hirelings. The
problem is that these verses in John 10 have been mischaracter-
ized. For too long we have identified the "thief" in verse 10 as
Satan. Jesus is talking about men who will "steal, kill, and destroy."

Let me start by saying that the one who "steals" abandons
the sheep at their moment of need. The image that comes to
my mind is the ministers that encourage you to give your "seed
offerings" that you might get blessed. They disregard the fact
that the word "seed" never refers to money in the Word of
God.

For example "seed" in the New Testament is the Greek word, *sperma*, and has the following uses, (a) agricultural and botanical, (b) physiological, as in Hebrews 11:11, and (c) metaphorically and by metonymy for offspring or posterity. The latter is the one used the most. I emphasize the word used is posterity not prosperity. Why do they insert the references to money? In the words of the Lord, "they care not for the sheep," or in most cases they are deceived themselves. I pray that they are guilty of the latter, for if they are guilty of the former, then the words "kill" and "destroy" best describes their motives.

To "kill" in the context of the Lord's words is the Greek word *thuo*, denoting to offer first fruits to a god. In other words, they get a victim prepared to be a sacrifice to a god. This god is themselves. This is relevant, if you want to understand how the word "kill" precedes "destroy." The targeted victim is then targeted to be "destroyed." That is the Greek word, *apollumi*, that is to be destroyed utterly, or to perish. The idea here is not extinction, but ruin and loss of well-being. They are lost from the real Shepherd. They will suffer the loss of well-being, as in the case of the unsaved, or lost as in John 3:16, or face the inevitable judgment.

> *Of how much sorer punishment, suppose ye shall he be thought worthy, who hath trodden under foot the Son of God and hath counted the blood of the covenant, wherewith he was sanctified, an unholy thing, and hath done despite unto the Spirit of grace?* (Hebrews 10:29).

The abundant life that the Lord wants his faithful to experience can be seen in the words of David,

> *Delight thyself also in the Lord; and he shall give thee the desires of thine heart* (Psalm 37:4).

The *American Heritage Dictionary* describes "delight" as

116

"something that gives great pleasure or enjoyment." As in life, while the expectations in Psalm 37:4, sounds simple, the difficulty comes in "delighting thyself also in the Lord." The Lord must become our greatest source of pleasure and joy. For then we can say,

When I cry unto thee, then shall mine enemies turn back; this I know for God is for me (Psalm 56:9).

There shall no strange god be in thee; neither shall thou worship any strange god. I am the Lord thy God, which brought thee out of the land of Egypt; open thy mouth wide and I will fill it. But my people would not hearken to my voice; and Israel would none of me (Psalm 81:9-11).

Let us learn from the real-life trials of Israel. Let us not follow after strange gods. Let us follow the true God by faith!

How can these "strange gods" a.k.a. apostates amass such large followings and work the works they do, including some apparent miracles? Let me give an answer that is stated in the Bible,

And you hath he quickened, who were dead in trespasses and sins; wherein in time past ye walked according to the course of this world, according to the prince of the power of the air, the spirit that now worketh in the children of disobedience (Ephesians 2:1).

Here Paul speaks of the spirit of this age. This is also a criticism of today's church. The devil takes the dead material (we were once dead in trespasses and sin), and he energizes us. The "prince of the powers of the air" worketh (energizes) in the sons of disobedience. This is why cults are as busy as bees and with the same result. The short of it is that false religions put the Body of Christ to shame with their zeal. Their lord, Satan, energizes them, while the Church is in a rest mode.

117

The psalmist asks a question,

If the foundations be destroyed, what can the righteous do? (Psalm 11:3).

Jude gives the answer, after telling us that we must contend for the faith;

Keep yourselves in the love of God, looking for the mercy of our Lord Jesus Christ unto eternal life. And of some have compassion, making a difference; and others save with fear, pulling them out of the fire; hating even the garment spotted by the flesh. Now unto him that is able to keep you from falling, and to present you faultless before the presence of his glory with exceeding joy. To the only wise God our Savior, be glory and majesty, dominion and power, both now and ever. Amen. (Jude 21-25).

And I will add, keep on believing. After all, it takes faith to believe and Faith Came.

Chapter 15

The War of Faith, Part 2

And these all having obtained a good report through faith, received not the promise; God having provided some better thing for us, that they without us should not be made perfect (Hebrews 11:39).

Upon these verses hinge the transition from the 5th dispensation of faith to the 6th dispensation. "These" in the 39th verse have been said to refer only to those who are represented to have suffered for their faith, as opposed to those who experienced victory over their trials. The troubling phrase is "received not the promise." However, the contrast is not between the two for they were all worthy of recognition. It is the antithesis between the ancient economy and the believers in the new economy or dispensation. All those whose are honorably recorded in this chapter of Hebrews, either expressly on account of their suffering on behalf their faith, or on account of their achievements, which relate to their faith—"all these received not the promise."

This is the promise of the resurrection to eternal life. For, as I have stated earlier, they could not obtain it because faith had not come. That is, the Author of our faith had not yet purchased our eternal destiny. That could not happen until Jesus Christ declared,

When Jesus therefore had received the vinegar, he said it is finished; and he bowed his head and gave up the ghost (John 19:30).

For the purpose of establishing consistency, let me call this 6th dispensation the time for the warriors of faith to do their thing. We are presently being watched by our predecessors, as Hebrews predicts:

Wherefore seeing we also are compassed about with so great a cloud of witnesses, let us lay aside every weight and the sin which doth so easily beset us, and let us run with patience the race that is set before us. Looking unto Jesus the author and finisher of our faith; who for the joy that was set before him endured the cross, despising the shame, and is set down at the right hand of the throne of God (Hebrews 12:1-2).

And the object of these activities is described as the faith (*tes pisteos*), which is an expression used to sum up the entire Christian position. Upon further reflection, the descriptions, author (*archegon*) and finisher (*teleoiten*), are highly suggestive. Together they span the whole spectrum of the life of Jesus, in relation to our faith. While the word," author," may have the same sense of the word "founder," it is more meaningful to view the term as "leader," especially in light of Hebrews 2:10,

For it became him, for whom are all things and by whom are all things in bringing many sons unto glory to make the captain of their salvation perfect through sufferings.

Whereas, the apostle, knowing that Jesus was historically and physically present on the earth after those listed in the first 5 economies, nevertheless, He is regarded as inspiring the saints of old. Not only is Jesus Christ the subject of Scripture, from beginning to end, but He is its ultimate author;

Search the scriptures; for in them ye think ye have eternal life; and they are they which testify of me. And ye will not come to me, that ye might have life. I receive not honor from men. But I know you that ye have not the love of God in you. I am come in my Father's name and ye receive not; if another shall come in his own name, him ye will receive. How can ye believe, which receive honor one of another and seek not the honor that the cometh from God only? Do not think I will accuse you to the Father; there is one that accuseth you, even Moses in whom ye trust, for had ye believed Moses, ye would have believed me; for he wrote of me. But if you believe not his writings, how shall ye believe my words? (John 5:39-47).

I challenge you to consider the words of Irenaeus, who is called the "Midwife of the Christian Bible." He interprets what Jesus is saying as, "the writings of Moses are His words." Irenaeus then extends this to include "the words of the other prophets." He goes on to say, "If anyone reads the Scriptures in this way, he will find in them the Word concerning Christ and a foreshadowing of the new calling." That "new calling" my brothers and sisters, can be seen in Hebrews 11:40,

God having provided some better thing for us, that they without us should not be made perfect.

Meanwhile, the linking of "joy" with suffering echoes a constant New Testament theme that will resonate loudly in this 6th dispensation. Remember that on the eve of His passion, Jesus spoke of His joy and of His desire that His disciples should share of it,

These things have I spoken unto you, that my joy might remain in you and that your joy might be full (John 15:11).

And now come I to thee; and these things I speak in the world, that they might have my joy fulfilled in themselves (John 17:13).

This "joy" was dependent on the verb translated "looking to," in the direction of Jesus. It implies a definite looking away from others and directing one's gaze towards our Lord. This verb, *aphorontes eis,* suggests the impossibility of looking in two directions at once. Using the racing analogy, a runner is trained to focus on the finishing line if he is to perform at his maximum efficiency. I will add that this target, Jesus, must be knowable, and the apostle is exhorting his readers, as I do today, to fix their eyes on the most perfect example of manhood, "the man, Christ Jesus." I will further add that the faith is not only the object of Jesus' activities, but describes our Lord, Himself that is why Paul describes faith as having to come (Gal. 3:25).

Joy is connected to obedience in verse 2 of this 12th chapter of Hebrews, which presupposes a life of discipline. This is essential to the Christian life, yet it is virtually ignored by many of today's biblical teachers. Let us not be like the example that Paul gave Esau:

Lest there be any fornicator, or profane person as Esau, who for one morsel of meat sold his birthright. For ye know how that afterward, when he would have inherited the blessing, he was rejected; for he found no place of repentance, though he sought it carefully with tears (Hebrews 12:16-17).

We should notice the difference between those referred to above and those of us in the new order. The heroes of the past are to be seen as spectators, and we are to be seen as being in the arena. When he says that "we are surrounded by so great a cloud of witnesses," he assumes that the Christians are aware of the presence of the spectators. The word used here more closely resembles the word *martyr*, and yet the use of the imagery here presupposes the use of the word, *spectator*. Ideally, these "witnesses" are to be distinguished from the cavalier attitudes of those today whose only desire is to be entertained with thoughts of prosperity.

These witnesses who are still watching today have a hope "that they without us should not be made perfect." They are well qualified to inspire us because they bear witness to the faithfulness of God to sustain His people in all circumstances. The word "cloud" gives the imagery of a large host. And the following verses give the writer's opinion of the preparation necessary for enabling the contestants to start the race.

For consider him that endured such contradiction of sinners against himself lest be wearied and faint in your minds. Ye have not yet resisted unto blood, striving against sin. And ye have forgotten the exhortation which speaketh unto you as children, My son, despise not thou the chastening of the Lord, nor faith when thou art rebuked of him; For whom the Lord loveth he chasteneth, and scourgeth every son whom he receiveth. If ye endure chastening God dealeth with you as with sons; for what son is he whom the father chasteneth not? But if ye be without chastisement, whereof all are partakers then are ye bastards, and not sons. Furthermore we have had fathers of our flesh which corrected us and we gave them reverence; shall we not much rather be in subjection unto the Father of spirits and live? For they verily a few days chastened us after their own pleasure; but he for our profit, that we might be partakers of his holiness. Now no chastening for the present seemeth to be joyous, but grievous; nevertheless afterward it yieldeth the peaceable fruit of righteousness unto hem which are exercised thereby. Wherefore lift up

the hands which hang down and the feeble knees
(Hebrews 12:3-12).

• We are to resist unto blood.
• We are to strive against sin.
• We are to despise not the chastening of the Lord.
• We are to give reverence to the Lord.
• We are to lift up our hands in praise,
• We are to receive the peaceable fruit of righteousness.

What are those witnesses looking for? They are looking for
you and I to exhibit the joy that the benefactors of the grace of
God should have. Instead we have cheapened God's grace by
the callousness of the lives we live. While they died having "received not the promise," we of whom it could be said, "God
provided some better thing for us," do not appreciate the
things that God's grace has provided. If we did, the churches of
this world would need the fire marshals of their respective lands
to invoke the fire protective laws to keep the attendance down
to within the regulated amounts. Our churches would resemble
rock concerts in that the willing seekers of the Word of God
would be lined up outside for days just to get in. Instead of witnessing us drag into worship service late, they would watch us
unfolding our tents that have been set up to insure all of us will
be able to participate in giving God His due praise.

We alone can sing "Blessed Assurance." We alone can be
saved, regardless of our unfaithfulness. We alone can worship
Jesus, not only as Messiah, not only as the Christ, but as the
Son of God. Only we, by faith, can fully appreciate the significance of the following words,

*For unto us a child is born, unto us a son is given and the
government shall be upon his shoulder and his name shall
be called Wonderful, Counselor, the mighty God, the everlasting Father, the Prince of Peace (Isaiah 9:6).*

Only we, by faith, would capitalize the word "son" in the above verse. He is the Son that God gave to make our faith complete. Now let us make use of the "better thing" so that they, the witnesses can be "made perfect."

Speaking of witnesses, we can see the consistency in the messages of some future witnesses. Watch and notice the answer God gives to their call of impatience:

> *And they cried with a loud voice saying How long, O Lord, holy and true dost thou not judge and avenge our blood on them that dwell on the earth? And white robes were given unto every one of them; and it was said unto them that they should rest yet for a little season until their fellow servants also and their brethren, that should be killed as they were should be fulfilled* (Rev. 6:10-11).

I pray that this chapter has closed the books on those who claim that we will not suffer for our faith. Faith had come by that time far into the future, however, the price had to be paid remained the same. They had the "better thing," but the time was not yet "made perfect."

Chapter 16

The Overview and Destination of Faith

Faith in God involves right belief about God. The word "faith" in ordinary speech covers both the credence of propositions ("beliefs") and confidence in a person or thing. In the latter case, some belief about the object trusted is the logical and psychological presupposition of the act of trust itself. Trust in a thing reflects a positive expectation about its behavior; rational expectation is impossible if the thing's capacities for behavior are even remotely unknown. Throughout the Bible, trust in God is made to rest on belief of what He has revealed concerning His character and purpose. In the New Testament, faith in God is synonymous with trust in Christ, as in John 14:1-14,

> *Let not your heart be troubled; ye believe in God, believe also in me. Jesus saith unto him, I am the way, the truth, and the life, no man cometh unto the Father but by me. If ye had known me ye should have known my Father also; and from henceforth ye know him and have seen him. Jesus saith unto him, have I been so long a time with you and yet hast thou not know me, Philip? He that hath seen me hath seen the Father; and how sayest thou then. Shew us the Father? Believest thou no that I am in the Father*

126

*and the Father is in me? The words that I speak unto you
I speak not of myself; but the Father that dwelleth in me,
he doeth the works. Believe me that I am in the Father
and the Father in me; or else believe me for the very works'
sake. Verily, verily, I say unto you, he that believeth on me,
the works that I do shall he do also; and greater works
than these shall he do; because I go unto my Father. And
whatsoever ye shall ask in my name that will I do that the
Father may be glorified in the Son. If ye shall ask any
thing in my name, I will do it.*

Clearly, acknowledgement of Jesus as the expected Messiah
and incarnate Son of God is regarded as basic to our faith.
Significantly, faith in Christ can exist where information about
Jesus is incomplete, as in the case of the disciples of Apollos,

*And it came to pass that while Apollos was at Corinth,
Paul having passed through the upper coasts came to
Ephesus; and finding certain disciples, he said unto them,
have ye received the Holy Ghost since ye believed? And they
said unto him, we have not so much as heard whether
there be any Holy Ghost* (Acts 19:1).

However, acknowledgement of His divine identity and
Christhood must be affirmed.

*Who is a liar but he that denieth that Jesus is the Christ?
He is antichrist that denieth the Father and the Son.
Whosoever denieth the Son, the same hath not the Father
(but) he that acknowledgeth the Son hath the Father also*
(I John 2:22-23).

*For many deceivers are entered into the world who confess
not that Jesus Christ is come in the flesh; this is a deceiver
and an antichrist. Look to yourselves that we lose not those
things which we have wrought but that we receive a full*

127

reward. Whosoever transgresseth and abideth not n the doctrine of Christ hath not God. He that abideth in the doctrine of Christ, he hath both the Father and the Son (II John 1:7-9).

Without that acceptance of His divinity all that is possible is idolatry or the worship of a manmade unreality. Therefore we are warned in I John 5:21, "Little children, keep yourselves from idols." Amen.

In fact, the frequency with which the epistles portray faith as knowing, believing, and obeying "the truth" shows that the biblical architects regarded orthodoxy as faith's fundamental ingredient:

But though we, or an angel from heaven, preach any other gospel unto you than that which we have preached unto you, let him be accursed. As we said before, so say I now again. If any man preach any other gospel unto you than that ye have received, let him be accursed (Galatians 1:8-9).

Paul, a servant of God and an apostle of Jesus Christ, according to the faith of God's elect and the acknowledging of the truth which is after godliness. In hope of eternal life, which God, that cannot lie, promised before the world began (Titus 1:1).

But we are bound to give thanks always to God for you, brethren beloved of the Lord, because God hath from the beginning chosen you to salvation through sanctification of the Spirit and belief of the truth (II Thess 2:13).

Seeing ye have purified your souls in obeying the truth through the spirit unto unfeigned love of the brethren, see that ye love one another with a pure heart fervently. Being born again, not of corruptible seed, but of incorruptible, by the word of God, which liveth and abideth for ever (I Peter 1:22).

Likewise, receiving the truth is synonymous with the born again experiences.

Then said Jesus to those Jews which believed on him. If ye continue in my word then are ye my disciples indeed; and ye shall know the truth and the truth shall make you free (John 8:31-32).

Faith also rests on divine testimony. Beliefs are convictions held on grounds, not of self-evidence, but of testimony. These beliefs should be treated as known certainties based on the worth of the testimonies on which they are grounded;

Beloved, now are we the sons of God and it doth not yet appear what we shall be; but we know that when he shall appear we shall be like him for we shall see him as he is (I John 3:2).

We know that whosoever is born of God sinneth not; but he that is begotten of God keepeth himself, and that wicked one toucheth him not. And we know the we are of God and the whole world lieth in wickedness. And we know that the Son of God is come and hath given us an understanding that we may know him that is true and we are in him that is true, even in his Son Jesus Christ. This is the true God and eternal life (I John 3:18).

More directly, the Bible views faith's convictions as certainties and equates them with knowledge because they rest on the testimony of a God who is immutable and cannot lie.

That by two immutable things in which it was impossible for God to lie we might have a strong consolation who have fled for refuge to lay hold upon the hope set before us (Hebrews 6:18).

In hope of eternal life which God that cannot lie, promised before the world began (Titus 1:1).

Therefore, Christians view their God as completely trustworthy; to do otherwise is to make God a liar.

He that believeth on the Son of God hath the witness in himself; he that believeth not God hath made a liar; because he believeth not the record that God gave of his Son (I John 5:10).

In addition, our faith rests on the recognition of apostolic and biblical testimony, which is as valid as God's own testimony to His Son. The supernatural aspects to faith rests on the ministry of the Holy Spirit. Because of sin and the work of the enemy, it is difficult for men to see and comprehend the teachings of the Bible and therefore they do not come to place their self renouncing trust in living Christ."

No man can come to me except the Father which hath sent me draw him; and I will raise him up at the last day. It is written in the prophets. And they shall be all taught of God. Every man, therefore that hath heard, and hath learned of the Father, cometh unto me (John 6:44).

Only by the grace of God and the ministry of the Holy Spirit can men be the recipients of this divine teaching and anointing which will allow them to believe in the Son and abide in Him.

But the anointing which ye have received of him abideth in you and ye need not that any man teach you; but as the same anointing teacheth you of all things and is truth, and is no lie and even as it hath taught you ye shall abide in him (I John 2:27).

God is the Author of all saving faith.

And in nothing terrified by you adversaries; which is to them an evident token of perdition, but to you of salvation and that of God. For unto you it is given in the behalf of Christ, not only to believe on him, but also to suffer for his sake (Phil. 1:28-29).

For by grace are ye saved through faith; and that not of yourselves it is the gift of God (Eph. 2:8).

The concept of biblical faith develops as God's revelation of grace and truth, on which faith rests, enlarges and is manifested in the person of Jesus Christ.

And the Word was made flesh and dwelt among us (and we beheld his glory, the glory as of the only begotten of the Father) full of grace and truth (John 1:14).

The Old Testament variously defines faith as resting, trusting, and hoping in the Lord, cleaving to Him, waiting for Him, making Him our shield and tower, and taking refuge in Him. The psalmists and prophets, speaking in individual national terms respectively, present faith as unwavering trust in God to save His servants from their foes and fulfill His declared purpose of blessing them. Isaiah, particularly, denounces reliance on human aid as inconsistent with trusting God.

Woe to the rebellious children, saith the Lord, that take counsel, but not of me; and that covering, but not of my spirit that they may add sin to sin; that walk to go down into Egypt and have not asked at my mouth; to strengthen themselves in the strength of Pharaoh, and to trust in the shadow of Egypt! Therefore shall the strength of Pharaoh be your shame, and the trust in the shadow of Egypt your confusion (Isaiah 30:1-3).

Meanwhile, the N.T. regards the self-despairing hope, world-renouncing, and heroic tenacity by which O.T. believers manifested as the model which Christians must reproduce. Christianity is avowed here, but also uniqueness; for each individual's faith is based on them receiving God's new utterances in the words and deeds whereby the faith of these O.T. saints becomes a barometer of present salvation:

> *God, who at sundry times and in diverse manners spake in time past unto the father by the prophets, Hath in these last days spoken unto us by His Son, whom he hath appointed heir of all things, by whom also he made the worlds; who being the brightness of his glory, and the express image of his person and upholding all things by the word of his power, when he had himself purges our sins, sat down on the right hand of the Majesty on high; being made so much better than the angels as he hath by inheritance obtained a more excellent name than they* (Hebrews 1:1-4).

Faith, in this dispensation, "came" with Christ; which is the subject of this book. The Gospels show Christ demanding trust in Himself as bearing the messianic message of the Gospel writers. John is the clearest proponent of this, emphasizing that faith ("believing on," "coming to," and "receiving" Christ) involves acknowledging Jesus' divinity, not merely accepting Him as a God-sent teacher and miracle worker, which has been shown to be insufficient.

> *Now when he was in Jerusalem at the Passover in the feast day, many believed in his name when they saw the miracles which he did. But Jesus did not commit himself unto them, because he knew all men, Jesus must be accepted as God incarnate* (John 2:23-24).

> *And Thomas answered and said unto him, My Lord and my God. Jesus saith unto him, Thomas, because thou hast seen me, thou hast believed; blessed are they that have not*

seen and yet have believed. And many other signs truly did Jesus in the presence of his disciples which are not written in this book. But these are written that ye might believe that Jesus is the Christ, the Son of God; and that believing ye might have life through his name (John 20:28-31).

And His atoning death is the sole means of salvation.

And as Moses lifted up the serpent in the wilderness, even so must the Son of Man be lifted up; that whosoever believeth in him should not perish, but have eternal life. For God so loved the world that he gave his only begotten Son, that whosoever believeth in him should not perish, but have everlasting life (John 3:14-16).

I am the living bread which came down from heaven, if any man eat of this bread, he shall live forever; and the bread that I will give is my flesh, which I will give for the life of the world. The Jews therefore strove among themselves, saying, how can this man give us his flesh to eat? Then Jesus said unto them, verily, verily, I say unto you, except ye eat the flesh of the Son of man, and drink his blood, ye have no life in you. Whoso eateth my flesh and drinketh my blood hath eternal life; and I will raise him up at the last day. For my flesh is meat indeed, and my blood is drink indeed. He that eateth my flesh and drinketh my blood dwelleth in me, and I in him. As the living Father hath sent me and I live by the Father, so he that eateth me, even he shall live by me. This is that bread which came down from heaven; not as your fathers did eat manna, and are dead; he that eateth of this bread shall live for ever (John 6:51).

Verily, verily, I say unto you, He that heareth my word and believeth on him that sent me hath everlasting life and shall not come into condemnation, but is passed from death unto life (John 5:24).

And this is life eternal, that they might know thee the only true God and Jesus Christ whom thou has sent (John 17:3).

While Paul shows that faith in Christ is the only way to a right relationship with God, Peter echoes this and presents faith as the dynamic hope and endurance under persecution. Let me close by reflecting back on this.

Women received their dead raised to life again; and others were tortured not accepting deliverance; that they might obtain a better resurrection. And others had trial of cruel mockings and scourgings, yea, moreover of bonds and imprisonment (Hebrews 11:35-36).

There is no doubt that the apostle here refers to the story that is recorded in the sixth and seventh chapters of the second book of the Maccabees. For the words are a summary of the things and sayings that are ascribed to Eleazar, who was beaten to death when he had been persuaded to accept deliverance by transgressing the law. And the same can be said of the mother and her seven sons, whose story and torments are also recorded. The words of Josephus are:

…they every day underwent great miseries and bitter torments; for they were whipped with rods and their bodies were torn to pieces, and were crucified while they were still alive and breathed.

When they were tortured, they would not accept deliverance, i.e., on the condition of their denying Jehovah and violating His law. When Eleazar was offered the means of escaping punishment, he replied, "It becometh not our age to dissemble. For the present time I should be delivered from the punishment of men, yet should I not escape the hand of the Almighty, alive and dead." When the youngest of the seven sons of the Jewish mother was assured by Antiochus, with an oath, "that he would make him both a rich and a happy man if he would turn from the laws of his fathers, and that also he would take him for a friend, and trust him with his affairs," he obstinately refused. And when the king ordered the mother to counsel the young man to save his life, her reply was, "I will counsel my son" and turning to her son, she said, "Fear not this tormentor, but, being worthy of the brethren, take thy death, that I may receive thee again in mercy with thy brethren."

We need more power to live our convictions. Where can we find it? By putting our faith in the Son of God:

> *Paul, a servant of Jesus Christ, called to be an apostle, separated unto the gospel of God, (which he had promised afore by this prophets in the holy scriptures). Concerning his Son Jesus Christ our Lord, which was made of the seed of David according to the flesh; and declared to be the Son of God with power, according to the spirit of holiness by the resurrection from the dead; by whom we have received grace and apostleship, for obedience to the faith among all nations, for his name. Among whom are ye also the called of Jesus Christ; to all that be in Rome, beloved of God, called to be saints. Grace to you and peace from God our Father and the Lord Jesus Christ* (Romans 1:1-7).

The word "designated" in verse 4 is used of Christ's appointment as judge of all. Paul does not mean that Jesus became the Son of God by the resurrection, but that He, who during His earthly ministry was the Son of God in weakness and lowliness, became by the resurrection, the Son of God in power. He then became both Lord and Christ.

Therefore let all the house of Israel know assuredly that God hath made that same Jesus, whom ye have crucified, both Lord and Christ (Acts 2:36).

In this position of power, it can now be said that "Faith Came." Let us not forget that before we get to that position, our faith must be found worthy. Or as Paul says,

For unto you it is given in the behalf of Christ, not only to believe on him, but also to suffer for his sake; having the same conflict which ye saw in me and now hear to be in me (Phil. 1:29-30).

Concerning the destination of "the Faith," let me share with you a spiritual principle: if you want to know what God will do in the future, then examine what He has done in the past. Paul confirms this when he said in Romans 15:4,

For whatsoever things were written aforetime were written for our learning, that we through patience and comfort of the scriptures might have hope.

Let us look at the plight of the Hebrew boys, who are referred to in Hebrews 11:34, "...Quenched the violence of fire..." There are two lessons that we can learn from their experiences that can help us today.

Wherefore at that time certain Chaldeans came near and accused the Jews. They spake and said to the king Nebuchadnezzar, o king, live forever. Thou, o king, hast made a decree, that every man that shall hear the sound of the cornet, flute, harp, sackbut, psaltery, and dulcimer, and all kinds of music, shall fall down and worship the golden image; and whoso falleth not down and worshippeth, that he should be cast into the midst of a burning fiery furnace. There are certain Jews whom thou has set over the affairs of the province of Babylon, Shadrach,

*Meshach, and Abednego; these men o king, have not re-
garded thee; they serve not thy gods, nor worship the
golden image with thou has set up. Then Nebuchadnezzar
in his rage and fury commanded to bring Shadrach,
Meshach and Abednigo. Then they brought these men before the king. Nebuchadnezzar spake and said unto them,
is it true O Shadrach, Meshach, and Abednego, do not ye
serve my god, nor worship the golden image which I have
set up? Now if ye be ready that at what time ye hear the
sound of the cornet, flute, harp, sackbut, psaltery, and
dulcimer, and all kinds of music, ye fall down and worship the image which I have made;; well, but if ye worship
not, ye shall be cast the same hour into the midst of a
burning fiery furnace; and who is that God that shall deliver you out of my hands? Shadrach, Meschach, and
Abednego, answered and said to the king, O
Nebuchadnezzar, we are not careful to answer thee in this
matter. If it be so, our God whom we serve is able to deliver us from the burning fiery furnace, and he will deliver us out of thine hand, O king. But if not, be it known
unto thee, O king that we will not serve thy gods, nor worship the golden image which thou has set up. Then was
Nebuchadnezzar full of fury, and the form of his visage
was changed against Shadrach, Meshach, and Abednego;
therefore he spake and commanded that they should heat
the furnace one seven times more than it was wont to be
heated. And he commanded the most might men that
were in his army to bind Shadrach, Meshach, and
Abednego, and to cast them into the burning fiery furnace* (Daniel 3:8-20).

Lesson #1, Consider that Daniel, the senior servant was
missing. Why? I believe that the "certain Chaldeans" chose a
time to accuse the Jews while Daniel was absent because they

knew that Daniel stood so high in the king's favor that they were fearful of the king's wrath if he came to Daniel's defense. So their attack was pointed at Shadrach, Meshach, and Abednego. From this I have learned that Satan, does not attack, contrary to popular opinion, the senior pastors as much as he focuses his attention on the less entrenched pastors and the beginning ministers, who are not yet settled in the Word. He will, through the Church, try to get them to conform to the traditions, already in place, or to get them to be numbered with the 10 disbelieving spies, rather than see them mature enough to be a Joshua or Caleb; to step out on their faith, even if it threatens their security.

Lesson #2, Let me quote Matthew Henry,

It was strange that Shadrach, Meshach, and Abednego would be present at this assembly, when it was likely they knew for what intent it was called together..."

Why did they not avoid the meeting? Think about this, it was already established that they would be as faithful to the king as much as possible. However, by faith they were willing to make a public stand against idolatry. And they were not satisfied enough to simply not bow down before the false god, but being in the position of power, they felt obliged to stand up against this type of gross idolatry. The challenge to those of us today who are in positions of power is will we bow before the idols of today, when we are apart from our mentors, or do we have faith enough to stand in the face of adversity. Faith has come.

To contact Dr. Johnson for further information or to book a speaking engagement, send an e-mail to:
ljoh478387@aol.com